the golden hour
book ii

Dedicated to the Forest volunteers,
and in memory of Ellie Maxwell

First published in Great Britain in 2009 by Forest Publications

First edition

10 9 8 7 6 5 4 3 2 1

ISBN-13: 978 0 9556456 3 1

Forest Publications
An Imprint of the Forest
Registered Office:
3 Bristo Place
Edinburgh
EH1 1EY
Registered at Companies House Edinburgh
Company Registration No. SC254177
Charity No. SC038234

Forest Publications is Magda Boreysza, Ericka Duffy, Jane Flett, Aiko Harman, Nick Holdstock, Martin McKenna, Benjamin Morris, Jason Morton and Ryan Van Winkle
Music editor: Gareth Warner
Cover and related artwork by Magda Boreysza
Art direction by Jason Morton
Additional design assistance from cyanblack and Artaxe
Typeset in Warnock Pro by Tactile Industries
Printed and Bound in Great Britain by Caric Press

A section of 'A Golden Bowl' by Nick Holdstock appeared in *Textualities* magazine

The publisher acknowledges support from the Scottish Arts Council toward the publication of this book

Scottish
Arts Council

CONTENTS

WHAT IS THE GOLDEN HOUR?

The Golden Hour is the first and last hour of light when everything glows warm: whether you're admiring an Afghan fort, undressing your lover, or retching on a bypass.

The Golden Hour is the space between sober and drunk, when everyone becomes funnier, more beautiful, and you couldn't imagine being anywhere else.

The Golden Hour is three simple chords, The Beach Boys seduced by Mungo Jerry.

The Golden Hour lasts as long as a cup of coffee, sipped alone on a Sunday morning, when the sun cracks through your kitchen window and you know the person in bed will wait.

The Golden Hour is throwing sticks to a dog that does not belong to you.

It is the curl of the tongue.

The Golden Hour is onions turning from white to caramel. It is holding hands; kissing; the ridge of her collarbone. The Golden Hour is milky. The bite of an axe into wood.

It is a sigh that lasts for days and heats the homes of the poor. It is red balloons in the toilet. Elephants. New jam.

Riding down a hill in the dark while a Serbian talks.

This is the Golden Hour.

Let us loosen our collars.

ERICKA
DUFFY

WHEN WE WERE BROKE

'By temperament I'm a vagabond and a tramp. I don't want money badly enough to have to work for it. In my opinion it's a shame that there is so much work in the world. One of the saddest things is that the only thing a man can do for eight hours a day, day after day, is work. You can't eat eight hours a day nor drink for eight hours a day nor make love for eight hours — all you can do for eight hours is work. Which is the reason why man makes himself and everybody else so miserable and unhappy.'

William Faulkner, *Paris Review Interviews, Volume II*

The house smelled of chocolate for a good few days after I made the cake. We ate pieces of it for breakfast, even when it went stale.

'We're broke till Wednesday' — that's how it went. We were holding out for Wednesday. We'd been broke since Tuesday. A week and a day. By broke, I don't mean, oh, we had a few hundred left on the overdraft, or we only had a twenty in our pocket. By broke, I mean, we had four quid between the two of us.

It had been seven quid on Thursday.

We didn't mind. We'd tell each other, we didn't mind. 'I don't mind that we have no money. Do you honey?' Grey would ask me, semi-rhetorically. 'What would we do with money?' I would answer.

I didn't tell Grey that there were a lot of things we could have done with money. We could have, for instance, bought five bags of marshmallows and toasted them in our fireplace. We could have bought a vintage, eggshell-green Hamilton Beach milkshake maker to make delicious milkshakes. We could have bought milk, full stop. We could have bought mussels and razorback clams from the fish store and had a steaming pot of fish on thick pieces of French baguette (we could have bought butter). We could have ordered a pepperoni pizza meal deal with chicken wings and a one-litre bottle of Coca-Cola. We could have had a bag of salt and vinegar crisps, a carton of Ben and Jerry's ice cream, and some sherbet fizzes.

I knew what Grey would say if I told him what we could buy. He'd tell me we already had food. We did. We had flour, oil, basmati rice, two cans of chopped tomatoes, one can of corn, three cans of baked beans, a bag of soft carrots. Our fruit bowl was dusty.

The condiments were gone. If the refrigerator could be classified according to feudal cataloging, the condiments were the vassals. They could only be usurped by cheese. The cheddar and brie were the lords and they were distant memories by Monday.

If we had money, Grey could buy a canvas that was already stretched for him, one that was adhered by nails that he didn't have to hammer himself. If we had money, he wouldn't be painting over 'The Lady With the Dog' right now. I loved 'The Lady With the Dog.' It had hung in our living room in three countries. I packed it with bubble wrap and masking tape. I carried it in my handheld luggage and forsook, say, my collection of seashells for 'The Lady With the Dog.' He painted it in Devonport, when we lived in New Zealand when we weren't broke. I would walk to Narrowneck beach with a blanket and a book and sit for the whole afternoon in front of Rangitoto. I'd take the shortcut through the labyrinth on the way home. He'd be covered in pink paint.

He could have painted over 'Mia', the big canvas of his ex-girlfriend. I've never met her. She hung in our hallway. The slip of her bra had fallen to her shoulder. She had clear green eyes. I've always inexplicably hated girls with green eyes. Mia was no exception.

When we had money, I made sure to stock up on canned goods, on sundries. I made Grey tote along our big suitcase on wheels to Lidl and I would buy ten cans of tomatoes, fifteen cans of baked beans, sacks of rice, tomato paste, and cubes of vegetable stock. Grey would chide me as we walked around the aisles, 'Do you think this is Paris in 1968?' He would roll his eyes as if I was going overboard. He preferred not to eat canned food. He preferred fresh, seasonal, local, organic, fair trade, stickered food that had a million antioxidant omega-3 something or others. He insinuated that my insistence on stockpiling was because of an innate North American hoarding mentality. We didn't discuss that further. This is because he was from England and I had plenty bad to say about that country. Besides, he loved Canada. For the most part.

At least it wasn't cold in the apartment, which it could have been. Our heat was on around the clock. It was February in Edinburgh and I watched pedestrians from the kitchen window. Everyone was bundled in layers. Opaque vapour streamed from their mouths. Since we'd been broke, bar the Thursday, I hadn't gone outside. 'Just come for a walk,' Grey would implore as he would put on his scarf, his gloves. I didn't because I had a fear that we'd walk somewhere and we'd need something, we'd need say, a glass of water, or a bandage, and we wouldn't be able to get one, because we had no money.

I've never not been broke so you would have thought that I would have gotten used to it. As a child, my sister and I never had the flashy snacks at recess. We would crave Fruit Roll-ups or chocolate bars. We'd seduce other little girls with charming manners only to get a taste of a grape Fruit Droplet. 'Why do you want that trash for, anyways?' Our mom would ask us and we had no answer. When we were old enough to stay at home alone, she stopped taking us along to the supermarket on her weekly visit. 'It's too traumatic,' she said. Every time we would walk down the cereal aisle Hyatia and I would throw ourselves on the ground and beg, literally beg, for Count Chocula or Lucky Charms.

'At least we have the heat,' Grey said and I agreed. We had the radiators going and he'd found two broken chairs on the road, beside the garbage bins and he brought them home to burn in the fireplace. We'd fall asleep drunk with warmth. And we were high, some of the time. There was the last of the pot that lasted till Saturday. We smoked the stems on the Sunday.

The heat was allowed to be on because the heating bill came the next week. By the next week, Grey's installment of his grant would clear. We could see the grant money in the bank, on the receipt the machine spit out at us. It said it was in the account already but the machine wouldn't let us take it out till Wednesday. When we pressed 'Cash Withdrawal' it said across the screen, 'Transaction Not Authorised/Available Balance: 0.' I thought it was funny that Scottish cash machines wrote '0' like that. I had not seriously contemplated of 0 as a number. I had thought of plus 0 or negative 0, but never had I thought of an unequivocal, straightforward 0.

I knew that Grey did not worry as to whether he was providing enough for me, as some gentlemen are prone to do regarding the domesticant, or regarding the woman they love, for that matter. Grey did not worry because he knew the whole sordid tale of my relationship with my ex-boyfriend Simon. In the apartment I shared with Simon, I watched a man from the electricity company scurry up a pole like a monkey, open a white box, and flick a switch that made our lights and fridge extinguish. I had picked up the telephone one day and heard an eerie silence. We had pulled the BBQ in the living room. We boiled our water for tea on it.

Grey knew how much I could endure. I think that is part of the reason he loved me.

On Thursday night I decided on a chocolate cake. I didn't consult Grey because the door to the living room was closed and his music was going at full blast. We gave each other space. We didn't have jobs, not the real 9-5 kind of jobs, but we had a work ethic, we had routines. I would work on a poem in the nook in the kitchen. He'd paint in the living room. Before the grants came, I'd hear him talking to his mom on the telephone. He'd try to convince her, 'But I am working. I'm just not being paid.' Those nights, in bed, he would go over all the reasons why he couldn't have a normal job. One was that he couldn't bear to be apart from me for 8.5

hours every day.

I took three pounds out of the collection of change on the hallway table. I put on a hat and took the house keys. On most days, we would go to a lovely fruit and vegetable stand that stocked heirloom tomatoes, pomegranate juice, avocados and artichokes. Grey bought these things called Goji berries that cost five pounds for a tiny punnet. He didn't even eat them. They went mouldy on the windowsill.

I went to Iceland, the budget supermarket. I'd never been in before. Grey vetoed Iceland. He hated big conglomerates in general and would eschew them for family-run shops. In a pinch, he may have deigned to go to Waitrose. When we first moved to Scotland, he gave me his opinion on the hierarchy of grocery stores. Iceland was dead last.

The store felt like a convergence of a hospital and a warehouse. It was a gargantuan, sterile box with fluorescent lights that coloured everyone who shuffled about inside with a blue hue. I picked up a wire basket at the entrance of the store. Yellow and red signs were hung from the ceiling announcing sales on Cadbury Cream eggs, on shrimp cocktail rings. Huge freezers lined each aisle. I walked slowly and looked into each. Frozen pizzas, frozen hors d'oeuvres, frozen hamburgers, frozen peas, frozen Yorkshire puddings were nestled inside. I trailed my finger along the glass lids of the freezers. It made a squeaky noise as I walked.

I went to the condiment aisle and saw the very same soy sauce that we used, the one that we bought for £3.99 at the fruit and vegetable shop. It was 99 pence at Iceland. I saw the same tomato paste, I saw the same balsamic vinegar, and I saw the same pesto. I estimated that we could save at least nine pounds on these few things, if we shopped here.

I put a little carton of milk, 100 grams of butter, a bag of sugar, and a box of hot chocolate powder in my basket. I walked over to the shelf of eggs. I could either buy six eggs for £1.50 or fifteen eggs for £1.00. The six were free-range, organic. Grey had told me, unequivocally, that he would never, not in his whole life, eat an egg that was not free-range.

'What if someone makes you eggs for breakfast at their house and you're a guest?' I asked.

'As long as I didn't know about it,' Grey answered, 'That would be fine.'

I stood for a long time at the egg stand. I handled the large plastic container of the 'Barn Eggs'. I handled the heavy (recycled) cardboard of the superior eggs. I made my choice and walked to the cash register. I averted my eyes from the Tunnock's teacakes, from the Walker's crisps, from the alcohol aisle that was populated by cheap knock-off versions (Baja Coconut Rum). I did not want to add any more items to the curious list in my head of the things I wanted but could not have.

There was a girl my age ahead of me. She was quick to put the little plastic stick in between my food and her food on the conveyer belt. I couldn't decide if her quickness was rude, or, antithetically, if it was overly polite. Maybe she felt she was doing me a favour. Or maybe it was just utilitarian. I looked at the things that she had chosen. An eight pack of Coca-Cola. One big block of Cadbury's chocolate. A big jar of Hellman's mayonnaise. A block of cheddar. Crisco oil. Tabasco sauce. Two cans of sardines. Two large bags of Hula Hoops. A pack of Toffee Crisp chocolate bars. A bag of Curly Wurlys. Four frozen pizzas. Pepperoni, Mozzarella, Barbequed Chicken, and Hawaiian.

She was a very slight girl. Skinnier than even I was. Shorter too. I couldn't imagine all of that stuff fitting into her. Just when her last item had been rung through, her hand lazily settled on a bag of liquorice all-sorts. They were in the point-of-purchase zone; in that space where chewing gum, single chocolate bars, Tic Tacs, beef jerky, and batteries congregate.

The all-sorts on the bag looked so enticing. The multi-coloured sandwiches looked like the perfect platonic representation of candy — the candy that I had always imagined in my head after watching *Charlie and the Chocolate Factory* when I was seven. Candy never actually did look like it did in that film. It was the same with highballs and cocktails. When we were young, Hyatia and I would watch old movies on channel two when our mom was working. We didn't have cable. That's the only channel we could get. Starlets would order Singapore Slings, Blue Lagoons, White Russians, Gin Rickeys, Tom Collinses. They would be brought on a silver tray by a waiter who wore a towel on his arm. Even in black and white, the colours of the drinks seemed technicolour; the glasses themselves seemed edible. When I got to the age that I could actually order them myself, the names were antiquated and bartenders had to consult a book before they presented me with my drink. They never tasted as good as I thought they would.

I tried to think of the last time I had eaten liquorice all-sorts. I couldn't place it. It then was my turn at the till; the woman had bagged all her purchases. The cashier dragged my items across a scanner and each beep seemed to be a warning. I considered then that I might not have enough money. Beep. Beep. Beep. I grew anxious and I tried to look at the total on the register (Beep) but there was nowhere that the subtotal was displayed. Right when I thought that the cashier would save me from this misery — she was scanning the last items — she asked if I had an Iceland card. I said no, and I got distracted because I was hurriedly doing math in my head whilst I was simultaneously watching an old man behind me, putting his goods on the belt. He had a bottle of one of the no-name whiskeys, and a single frozen chicken and mushroom pie. I put the piece of plastic on the belt and I smiled to show him, it's not that I want to segregate us, it's not that at all. This is just easier.

I had 50p left. I did not even think before I did what I did next. I grabbed a bag of liquorice all-sorts. I gave the cashier my remaining coin. I didn't take an Iceland bag. I put the goods in my big cloth purse. As I walked home, I saw the girl who was ahead of me in the cashier queue, at the bus stop. She was standing with a morbidly obese boy who may have been between the ages of five and fifteen. It was hard to gauge. The number 35 was in the distance. I heard her say, 'The bus is coming, we'll be home soon' and he said, 'But Mom, I want some chocolate now.' She was rustling in the white plastic Iceland bag as I turned the corner.

I felt a wave of panic as I turned the key in our lock. It was silent in the apartment. I had a fear that Grey would be in the hallway, or in the kitchen, scared he'd playfully say, 'Whatya got there?' I was frightened that he'd go through my purse, though he never had.

I went to the bedroom and gently stashed the purse in our closet. I walked down the hallway to the living room. The light was on. I was timid. I felt like I was walking into a meeting with the principal, or facing up to Mom when I cut off Hyatia's bangs with sewing shears, though it was Hyatia's own request. I knocked softly. There was no answer. I took a deep breath. I pushed open the door. Grey was sprawled across the couch. The room was warm with the fire. He was sleeping with a smile on his face.

Hurriedly, I went back to the closet and grabbed my purse. I brought it into the kitchen. I decanted the sugar into our sugar bowl. I took out a mixing bowl and I emptied the milk into it. I unsheathed the butter and put it in our butter dish. I cut off half and put it in a small bowl. I opened the plastic pack and I took out the eggs. I stored six behind the bag of flour in our pantry. I opened a cupboard that we put our glass bottles in, ostensibly to be recycled. We hadn't yet gone to the glass-recycling depot once since we had moved into the apartment six months before. The cupboard was bursting with pickle and mustard jars, with Bombay Sapphire, whisky, beer and soy-sauce bottles. I scattered six other eggs around the bottles.

I cracked three and put them in with the butter. I added the hot chocolate. I added the sugar only after I had taken all the packaging downstairs to the communal garbage bin. I threw in the plastic egg container with the garbage. I ran back upstairs before I started to feel guilty about that. I should have walked the ten meters further and put it in the recycling bin.

Grey woke later and the chocolate cake was done, cooling on a wire rack. He walked into the kitchen. His hair was tousled, his eyes were puffy. His face was lined with the indentations of the couch cushion. I did what I think should be done to anyone who is soft with sleep, to anyone who cannot clench a fist because their hands are still too weak. I walked over to where he stood and I hugged him.

'Is that a chocolate cake?' he asked.

'I took three pounds,' I said.

'You made a chocolate cake with three pounds?' he mused, and he seemed far away, as if he was still dreaming, as if in the dream I was both me and at the same time not me, like when you are in a house, that you know in the dream is your house, which is not, in real-life, your actual house.

'I always think, you know, that you're somehow magical. I always forget that you can do these things, that you are resourceful. I always forget that about you. How you do these things. How you manage, when we have no money, how you manage to make it all okay. I smelled chocolate cake when I was dreaming,' he said as he closed his eyes and breathed in.

His voice rang of truth, of something unsaid that we both knew to be honest. He looked at me like I was a faerie or a pixie, of someone who was unpinned to the realities of life. He thought I was like this because he was like this. He didn't like going to the post office. He didn't like paying bills. He didn't like counting money. It is not that he pretended that those things did not exist. He didn't allow them to exist, so they didn't.

When we played board games, like Monopoly, unlike in actual life, he was shrewd with his money whilst I spent mine haphazardly on the red properties, on the yellows, and on the railways because they're my favourites. He watched as I went bankrupt every time. He allowed me to make playful deals that deviated from the official rules. Contracts that involved me satisfying him in minor sexual acts.

But somehow his grant applications were sent. Somehow we still had a telephone. Somehow, we had flour, rice, and baked beans. Somehow we had a chocolate cake.

After this, after the chocolate cake, I never again made him come with me when I went to Lidl. I never again made him pull the suitcase. I never again allowed him to watch me internally haggle between one can of kidney beans over another.

He smelled like milk when we ate pieces of the cake, in front of the fire. It was the smell of sleep retreating.

'That was so good,' he said and leaned back contentedly.

'I got all-sorts too,' I told him.

'All-sorts? That liquorice candy?'

'Yeah,' I said and I got up and retrieved them. We ripped open the bag and ate them. We both got sugar headaches. This led to a nightlong conversation. We stayed up talking until we murmured. The sun came up. We talked about many things and nothing in particular. We didn't talk about how much we loved each other, about how we do things for each other all the time. We didn't talk about that because it seemed evident. It seemed a matter of course.

That chocolate cake got us through the next few days. In that time, Grey took down the canvas of Mia and put a thick layer of white gesso over it. I asked, 'Grey, don't you think you should wait till Wednesday? We'll be rich on Wednesday. You can buy a new canvas.' But he grunted in the way that he did when he didn't want to explain himself so I made no further comment on it. On Tuesday, we spent the last four pounds on a cheap bottle of red wine. By Wednesday, Mia and her green eyes had disappeared and a surreal painting of liquorice all-sorts was drying in the living room.

When he was ready to talk about it, it was a decade or so later, at a dinner party. He started, 'That painting is based on when we were broke,' and he covered my hand with his and continued, 'I mean, we were really broke, not like I don't have money to buy a video game broke,' and he looked particularly at our son Isaiah, who was eleven, or so, at the time, and Isaiah bristled slightly but I smiled warmly at him and he stopped because he was interested, we all were interested in what Grey had to say. He rarely talked like this. 'We had no money for anything and we were two waifs in the world. We didn't understand money; we didn't care about it at all. You wouldn't think, looking around you...' he gestured with his fork to our walls, to our table, 'but there was a time when we had ideals. Hestia,' he pointed to me, 'your mother,' he said to Isaiah, 'once used the very last of our money, the very last pennies that we had, not on a chicken, not on something practical like that. No, my lovely Hestia spent the money on a bag of all-sorts. And that's why I have loved her for so long.' This was a moment that doesn't happen often. This was a moment where everyone's eyes filled with liquid before they could even contemplate their tear ducts.

Then the moment passed.

Grey died not long after that night. It would be romantic to say that maybe he knew he was going to, maybe he had a premonition, and maybe that's why he explained that painting, his most famous one, one that he had never before commented on. Maybe that's why he explained his love for me, for the same reason, so that it could never be misunderstood.

But I know he couldn't have known. He couldn't have or he would not have taken his bicycle that day. He couldn't have or he never would have ridden down Easter Road that afternoon. He couldn't have known, I think, because if he did, he would have told me. He told me everything.

We found the eggs in the spring. We were finally going to pay our civic responsibility and wheel the bottles down the four or so blocks to the glass-recycling depot. I was rummaging in the closet for the suitcase on wheels. He was taking the bottles out of the cupboard and arranging them on the counter.

'Hestia,' he called out. When I came into the kitchen he was holding an egg in his hand.

'What are these doing here?'

I looked at him and said, 'I don't know.'

He looked at me with the kindest eyes. He said, 'Oh my lovely, only you would put eggs in with the bottles.'

ANDREW PHILIP

THE MELODY AT NIGHT, WITH YOU
ECM 1675

Snow bound and determined to break
out of the silence enforced by chronic fatigue
Jarrett is at his piano again   (the first time
in let's not contemplate how long for a man
as given to his art as this)   stripping
the tune right back to all that ever mattered,
taking it to heart the way you'd want
her to take what you know most sparing:
your softest, most unguarded speech and touch—
no smoke, no mirrors, no sleight of hand,
no firecracker runs or full-voltage solo virtuosics:
just the tune; the tune and Christmas coming.
A moment to warm the fingers. Press *RECORD*.

THE BIRLIN JAR

The yin in the faimly that got aw the curls,
ma skinnymalink brither

wid pace the village, daunerin here an there
by his lane

or wi me an the dug in the efternuin,
swingin his airms

an rockin. Awbody kent him. Awbody kent
he wis hairmless,

sae think on the rage A felt when the gang
o aulder laddies

that aye plowtered by the phone box
skraiched efter him

Keith—pu yer trousers doun! Yer mammy tellt ye
tae pu yer trousers doun!

an me nae mair nor a bairn out wi him an the dug
by ma lane.

Revenge cam, doucelike enough, fae ma brither's
uncanny, yissless skeel:

tae tip a jam jar ontae its lip and haud it
birlin for meinits.

Seein thae laddies' faces when they'd aw tried
an cuidnae even

get stairtit fair made the hert in me yell
Gaun yersel! Ya beautae!

WATERGAW
FOR EILISH BETHAN PHILIP

Let her wake to
    a city cleansed
        and glistening:

each block and landmark
    immersed and raised up
        while she slept

each foot- and tyreprint
    named and kissed for
        the saint who made it.

Though she—like Noah—
    may be uncertain
        of the sky's intent,

let her breathe
    the freshness
        after this flood—

each breath lighter
    than God's touch
        on a sheltered pool.

JANE GRIFFITHS

LESSONS FROM MY FIRST GIRAFFE
FOR NIGEL AND HILARY

The habits of camouflage.
How to approach a mezzanine.
How to articulate at the knee delicately as a lady
                    stepping down from her carriage.
A preference for what's out of reach.
How to trust the improbable.
Vertigo, or a warped sense of perspective.
How to wink, slowly.
How to curl my lip to the shape of a leaf.
How to keep my feet on the ground in Gandy Street
while still stretching languidly to graze the long slopes
round Rougemont Castle where goldfish swim
star-like in the bowl of the hill.
A fondness for marmite.
The fissure between the parts and the whole.

LAWS OF PHYSICS

That whole drive south through the worst floods on record
(the M1 closed, the A1 closed, windows the length of Pocklington
outed by a bow wave and the A19 silver in the rear view),
that whole two days of it I had in mind the shape of your hands
caged on the car's radiator as if it were a live thing, and how
you asked sidelong if I'd even the faintest inkling of the laws
of thermodynamics.

I felt the pull.

I could have turned back, I could have driven on water
past the fast-flowing villages, the beached cathedrals
and all the collateral damage, past the last cafe in England,
the B-roads clinging to their ledges, the pines with wingspans
like broken signposts sloping off across the border and the final
pass where the whole country falls away vertiginously as the sheer
sheet of water off a duck's back when it lifts into the unfathomable air
and to the north there's just the windscreen tilted against the sky,
the horizon like a hint of space between two hands, not quite touching.

Think of it, the distance between where we are and where we might have been.
The faultline between an idea and the grounds for it.
The way a postcard takes six weeks to arrive.

Still, we've our hands and our keyboards and their letters without strings;
we've swapped notes on apple trees, the habits of the birds—

though I've yet to mention the mineshaft that's split my garden
and how the fruit that falls there must spin crimson ellipses
in darkness as it slips blindly through the well of the earth—
or just how often I'll catch myself

listening for the splash.

ST STEPHEN PLACE

The chair around you is enormous as the broad
white margins of the book you hold defensively as a shield
with its centrepiece of a chair, and a child learning

the habit of putting words to things like pins
puckering a paper pattern, the thin sound of the rain.

Over the page you find there's a boy at the window
watching two pigeons turn and turn about on the clothes line,
hearing the neighbours overhead crank up for their nightly

argument with all the fanfare of a primitive gramophone
(*huffa, puffa, arsehole*).
                        And all of you waiting for a turn
in the weather, for snow. For something concrete.

Tomorrow the mountains could be hunched above the town
that today runs out for miles to meet them. Tomorrow
the snow could lie like a habit: as quiet and unassuming.

For now you stand distracted, with the real child,
the imagined story, the upstairs neighbours carrying on
in ways that don't bear repeating.

Where will you turn? Will you carry on reading?

SPENCER
THOMPSON

PANCAKE, AM I A BASTARD?

'*Flummoxed*!' said Brian. 'I'm *flummoxed*!' Brian had read his dad's diary, read the words, 'I want to learn a new word every day', and co-opted the idea as his own, having looked up the word *co-opted* in his electronic dictionary. It was only with the passing of time he realized he'd *co-opted* the word *co-opted*. Could a person be more *flummoxed* instead of merely *flummoxed*? *Flummoxed*-er? He hid the book behind his dresser and sighed, in what he would have described as a particularly *artesian* sigh, if asked. His dad was still dead, after a week, his mom still slept, after a week. Her hair had turned gray almost overnight. He counted the *compounding* number of grays as she slept. The doctor had given her pills which he said would make her better, but which Brian suspected only made her sleep more. He almost thought he could see a single strand turn from black to white, almost thought he saw the change from sorrow to better. 'Are you better?' he asked. She didn't answer. He'd almost forgotten it was Saturday. He could watch cartoons.

She'd pulled into the driveway too fast, plowing into his dad as he passed by pushing the mower. 'Is life a *transitive* thing?' asked Brian as he fixed himself breakfast, pouring cereal, milk; pausing to stare up at the ceiling, at the pancake he'd tried to flip in the pan several days before. 'I aimed too high.' Pancake didn't say anything, just stared back at him from above. If a word could describe Pancake, Brian believed it might be *obstinate*. He remembered being sick the year before, his mom making him pancakes the first day he'd woken up, back from the hospital, flipping them high, higher. Highest yet, he had said. 'Flip it higher than the highest high ever went high.' She had. Staring up at Pancake, stuck to the ceiling, blackened and charred on one side, raw and sticky on the stuck side, made Brian feel low.

'Am I an orphan?' he asked Pancake. He'd heard orphans were bastard children. Older kids at the playground told him that. He had looked up bastard and orphan on his electronic dictionary. His dad had given Brian the dictionary just hours before he'd been hit by the family's Volvo — a car his dad had assured his mom was the safest on the market after crash tests. He was pronounced dead by the postman delivering their mail at the time, the sirens of an ambulance heard in the distance. They could never have arrived in time. The package containing Brian's telescope was still on the kitchen table. He'd waited weeks for that package, but now didn't feel like exploring anything, seeing if the man in the moon actually existed. Pancake was real enough, and didn't require a telescope. If he had had a father, then didn't have a father, was he now a bastard? Could you become a bastard? If you were a son and then a father, did you become a bastard when you were no longer a son? Or became a father?

'Oh, Calgon, take me away,' Brian yelled. That's what Nancy's mom said. Nancy was his best friend, and the only person who had both kicked him and then kissed him where she kicked him. Nancy said that her mom, whenever she got frustrated, would throw back her head, roll her eyes, and say 'Calgon, take me away.' Nancy was at summer camp. Brian met her in first grade the year before. She'd moved in next door but he hadn't met her until recess that first day back from being sick. Their class had played Red Rover, Red Rover, the game where you try to run through held hands of people standing in a line. Nancy had crashed through him, not past either of the hands he held, and, knocking him to the ground, said, 'My name is Nancy; I live right next door to you. I'm glad you're not dead.'

The phone rang. Was it one of those old women from church? They stopped by every day, leaving casseroles. He could never tell them apart. He tried to find out by what color coat they wore, but each of them wore purple coats. He asked one yesterday if she was a member of the purple coat club. She patted him on the head, told him to be a good boy and be sure to bake that particular dish at four hundred degrees for one hour. He left the casseroles on the kitchen table, next to his telescope. He preferred cereal. Cat, his cat, ate the uncooked dishes, licked them clean. Actually, Cat was asleep now, as well, and had been for several days. When Brian poked it, Cat didn't move. Brian had read that animals could be male or female, but it seemed a *gross invasion* for him to check whether Cat was a boy or a girl. It might be a bastard, as well.

He picked up the phone and said, 'Hello, this is Brian.' There was a long pause. Brian wondered if his grandma had fallen asleep on the phone again. She had *narcolepsy*. She sometimes couldn't walk straight.

'Could I please speak with the man of the house?' came the voice from the other end.

'You're not grandma,' said Brian.

'Is the man or head of the household available?'

'Well, I guess I'm the man in this house, or I could be a bastard. I'm not sure.'

'…Are you satisfied with your current long distance service?'

Brian thought about the line strung between his window and Nancy's, several hundred feet away. They talked every night when she was home into empty chilli cans, their voices stretching hundreds of feet.

'Well, no I'm not. Could you make my line go to Maine? That's where Nancy is. I might need more twine. Do you know how far Maine is from here?'

'We'll call back later.'

'But…'

It was no use, the man had hung up. Brian still didn't know how far away Maine was. He lived in Connecticut, which he was told was a suburb of The Big Apple. Why name a city after a fruit? When he asked Nancy this, she'd simply kicked him again.

'Pancake, people are stupid,' Brian declared. 'Mom ran over dad, she won't wake up, Cat's sleeping, too. I don't know how far away Maine is, the women in the purple coat club want to know if I've brushed my teeth and said my prayers.' Brian stuck out his tongue. That's what he'd tell the women who knocked on his doors and left casseroles which made Cat fall asleep and go stiff. His cereal had gotten all soggy.

Brian spent the morning playing sock puppets and talking with Nancy, though she wasn't there. 'How's Maine, silly billy bo-billy?' Nancy's puppet sock would have kicked him, he just knew it. Nancy was a kicker, but Brian still liked her.

Cartoons were over; that meant one thing: lunchtime. Time for cereal. Brian had seven bowls of cereal yesterday, and was on his third bowl today. He was going to need a lot more milk if he was going to eat anymore. Eating cereal dry was what birds did. He counted twenty-three quarters from his money jar, and then climbed out his window, swung out and into the maple tree that was perfect for climbing, and scrambled to the ground. It was his *preferable* way of leaving the house. He often ran upstairs and climbed down instead of simply opening the door and strolling out.

Mr. Lanski was taking his daily walk. He was strangely frozen in his left side, and according to what Brian had heard, took a daily walk for his constitution. He walked with a thrust, throwing his left side forward with each step. Mr. Lanski had told Brian that his way of walking was because he was training for a future career as a boxer, but Brian didn't quite believe him.

Brian knew what a *constitutional* was. Mr. Lanski often got lost after he returned from the hospital. He had to take his walks in front of the house, and often ended up next door at Brian's place, wondering where he was. Brian walked him home lots of times. Mrs. Lanski gave him quarters and said things like, 'Well, thanks for getting that old man home in time for lunch. You need a tip and a PB&J.' In order for Mr. Lanski to remember to walk the prescribed distance the doctor recommended, he walked from the beginning of his lawn to the edge of Brian's lawn, dropped a rock, then turned around and walked back, until there were two piles of twenty rocks on either side of his property. Brian got quarters every time he picked up the rocks and placed them in a small box on the Lanskis' front porch. Picking up rocks was what paid for his new unopened telescope, and would pay for the milk he was going to buy.

Brian waved to Mr. Lanski, then turned and began walking in the other direction, towards Giant T, a small grocery store that sold cheap Valentine's Day chocolate year round, and had a small ice cream bar inside. It was probably one of his favorite places in the world. Where else could you get bubble gum ice cream with real bubble gum? When Nancy and he ate it, their tongues turned blue. She could touch her nose with her tongue, and did exercises to stretch it more, and they would argue who had a bluer tongue.

Giant T was on the other side of the busy street near his house. He knew to look both ways twice before crossing. Several years ago, the Lanskis' daughter had been killed when a drunk driver passed out at the wheel. She'd been in a coma for a month before passing on, as Brian had been told, which meant die. Brian had seen an aged newspaper article posted on the Lanskis' refrigerator, held by a pink and blue butterfly magnet, a picture of a Camaro smashed against a cracked telephone pole.

When he asked Mrs. Lanski about the picture, she'd kissed him on the top of his head and said that in order to remember the good, sometimes you had to remember the bad. Was that what she had said? Sometimes adults made no sense. Brian always wondered if their daughter liked bubble gum ice cream, too. The light turned into walk and looking both ways — twice — he skipped across the street.

He could skip *like mad*, which he knew to be a British saying, from the Sixties, when people would say things like 'That's groovy, baby,' or 'I can dig it.' There was a picture of his dad at something called Woodstock, next to his mom, both of them wearing flowers in their hair, which was long, his dad holding what he referred to as a 'jay', which Brian knew to be an illegal *narcotic*. They would sometimes have an extra glass of wine at dinner, and his mom would go sit in his dad's lap and they'd imitate their old selves, laughing and talking slang from their hippie days, before Brian. They had a Volkswagen van and everything, played guitar, were arrested for sitting in places. Then, they told Brian, they had to join the real world, and got jobs. He didn't understand any of it, just that he could skip like mad, and did so across the intersection. He skipped all the way across the parking lot. He jumped on one foot around a concrete barrier. Brian's dad had said he was the best jumper he'd ever seen.

Brian liked the idea of his dad looking down from heaven — wasn't heaven always up? Well, he knew that his dad could see him jump. His dad could brag about it to all the other dead people up there. Alice Lanski, his grandparents — well, except his grandma with narcolepsy, his goldfish Sniffles. It was a funny idea that a goldfish could have the sniffles. He waved up in the air, then winked up in the air — his dad would think that was funny, but it made Brian feel sad so he walked into the store. He didn't want his dad to see him cry, or anyone else. He pretended to have something in his eyes — sleep boogers, or a migraine, just like the ones Nancy's mom used to get. Especially after Nancy's dad left home.

Down in the dairy section, he selected one gallon of two percent milk. Three dollars, twelve quarters. That left more than enough for an ice cream cone of rainbow sherbet and bubble gum. He always looked at all the flavors and picked the same one or two. Bubble gum if he had enough money for one scoop, and rainbow sherbet as well if he had enough for two. It was cool to look at all the flavors, but he could never understand why someone would buy coffee ice cream. That was gross.

He sat outside on a rocking horse which cost a quarter to ride, not riding it, just eating his ice cream, until some kid with a runny nose came up and said 'Mommy, he's not even riding it, he's just hogging it.' Brian got off to let the kid ride the horse. He was down to the cone anyway, in some ways the best part of the ice cream, as long as it hadn't gotten soggy. Soggy things weren't good. Soggy cereal, soggy ice cream cones, and *inversely*, a word he knew to mean exactly opposite, stiff things, like Cat on the kitchen table, his father lying in the casket looking so formal and dignified, not at all like who he was, those were also bad, which was *synonymous* with not good.

He hopped on the other leg back across the parking lot, looked both ways, waited for the light, and skipped across — like mad, not mad in a crazy or a good way, but like he was mad. He skipped in anger.

'Stupid people who hit little girls with their cars, and stupid accident that killed dad.'

Brian knew that he probably looked like a madman to all those passengers in cars stopped at the light, like those people who walk down the street muttering to themselves in big cities he'd seen. New York, San Francisco. His grandma lived in San Francisco. He stomped each skip, and probably didn't even look like he was skipping. He put his arms out in front of him like he was a dinosaur, like a T-Rex or a zombie. It was hard work carrying a gallon of milk with his arms held out in front of him, and Brian was certain that T-Rexes didn't stomp around carrying milk in their skinny arms.

When he got home he put the milk in the fridge and tip-toed into his parents' room. His mom was still asleep. Brian knew his mom got up every night to check on him, and then went back to sleep, taking another pill and washing it down with a glass of water. There were seven empty glasses next to the sink. Brian counted each glass as they gathered, pointing to each and saying Monday, Tuesday, Wednesday... as if to say good morning before he ate a bowl of cereal. He always pretended to be asleep, like he did when his parents fought and he didn't want to hear. Brian knew it was probably *ludicrous*, but what if he kept so quiet that he could hear them argue again, and then be so happy?

He held his breath when she came into his room and looked at him sleeping. She left notes: I think Cat might be dead, Brian; or, Sorry Brian, I'm just really tired. Brian knew that eventually she would sleep away her tiredness. He was once really tired himself, and everything became blurred and he had been so hot, and then so cold. Later they told him that his temperature had been 106, and the doctors put him in ice to cool him. He'd slept for two weeks and it seemed both a long time and no time at all, but he could move again, and he was hungry! He'd heard funny voices, far away — foggy voices. There was some sort of continuous beep, beep, beep, the words 'stat this' and 'stat that.' There were murmurs and chairs that squeaked, little pinches in his arms, flashes of light in his eyes, the word *meningitis*. That was a disease.

'That's okay, mom,' he whispered. Afternoon cartoons were about to start. Brian felt hungry. He felt like having a bowl of cereal. Cat was beginning to stink a little bit. Cat needed a bath. There was time enough for that after cartoons were over. After he had picked up Mr. Lanski's rocks.

JULIA
BOLL

A HOUSE IN DISORDER

I am in the tower loft, my right cheek pressed against the window to feel it tremble in the storm, when the bell rings. I open my eyes but remain crouched against the glass, wishing the intruder to leave; they should have learned by now that I am not to be disturbed, that I am busy.

The bell sounds again, and I pull away from the smooth glass. My cheek has left a damp mark which gleams in the lamplight. I try to shake the up-surge of joy and thrill the bell brings with it, the urge to race downstairs and along the hall, to fling the door open, to find myself deceived, again.

Vowing to unscrew the bell and throw it away, I walk down the stairs, carrying the old lamp, dragging an army of silent shadows behind me to the ground floor and through the hall. I stop in front of the door and listen. Maybe they have gone away, maybe they have been worn out by the rain and by the storm-bride tearing out their hair.

There is a faint knock, timid even, and I wonder if the daring sound of the bell might have shaken the intruder's wish to disturb. They are persistent: another feeble knock begs through the wood, and by now I'm curious enough to see who would be so desperate to hover at this door in the middle of the night, 'past the witching hour' as John calls it, but I mustn't think of that now, or I'll have to curl up on the slates and moan.

I turn the lock and then remember the deadbolt. When I have hauled it out of the two rings, the door swings open towards me, inviting a gust of wet leaves and rain, and on the front steps there is something huddled against the doorframe, dirty and drenched, wrapped in a thin jacket.

When I raise my lamp, it turns its face towards me, which seems to be only eyes.

Le gosse.

He looks like a drowned kitten, the wet hair plastered around his face, a sodden scarf drenching his collar. We stare at each other, me incredulous, he imploring, and the next gust shoves him in over the threshold, stumbling into the hall in a flurry of decaying leaves. He catches himself against the coat rack, and I heave the door shut into the face of *la tempête* outside. We stand in the hall, at a distance of five metres, and silently measure each other up: me dumbstruck by his inexplicable appearance up here, and *le gosse* — he just gazes at me out of his wide eyes, shivering violently, his hair and clothes dripping all over the floor. Somewhere in the back of my mind float the questions I should probably ask, but I'm too weary for words tonight. I vaguely wonder where I saw him last and then remember: Easter, when we went down to attend the wedding of his sister, who is John's niece, and now it dawns on me that he must be here to see his uncle, and I resent him for making me think of John. I let him stand there and climb up the stairs, not looking back. I would not know what to do about him anyway.

I do not want to be bothered. I do not wish to be disturbed, I have things to do, I have memories to keep, I have my grief to attend.

This is a full-time occupation. *La tempête* completely threw me off schedule; I spent hours feeling her vibrate through the pane, decoding her howling and moaning as she tried to upturn the house, and now she has gone to singing sea-songs backwards and rattling at the window latches, looking for something she lost. I know the feeling. I step to the window again and press my palms against it.

'Whatever you are looking for,' I whisper, because we have spent so many nights together that we have grown quite intimate, 'if it is here, I won't give it back to you. Not until you return mine first.'

She withdraws for a second and I halt my breath. Then she launches a forceful attack against the shuddering windows, so that I can almost taste the seawater she has hurled upwards and thrown in for good measure. I defiantly lift my chin and stare at the darkness outside, because she has veiled the moon, to prevent me from seeing her. We are in for a long night, I realise, and pull my cardigan closer.

I wake up with a stiff neck, in the armchair by the window, as the sky turns a lighter shade of grey and the rain changes direction and drums against the shingles at an almost right angle. It sounds much more sober now than the frantic high pulse played out against the roof and the windows during the night. *La tempête* seems to sulk in a nest of dark clouds further north over the sea, which is a small victory for me, so I leave the loft and wander downstairs, towards the kitchen. I have an inexplicable sudden desire for breakfast.

In the hall, on the old sofa on the long side, there is a bundle of cloth, and it is breathing.

I had forgotten about *le gosse*.

I stop in the middle of the hall, glancing over, not sure whether it bothers me that he is still here or not. I step a bit closer, he is lying on his side, legs bent, and almost fully covered with a tatty red blanket that must have always been covering the sofa, I realise; it does look vaguely familiar.

I continue my way through the hall and into the kitchen, which has filled with the same colour of grey light I saw from the loft. The fridge hums lowly, and I hesitate, not remembering if the queasiness will go away if I force food down my throat, or if it will get worse. I haven't tried in a while. I find some milk in the fridge and pour a glass, setting it on the table and considering it. After three gulps I give up making myself drink it. I touch the back of John's chair and scald my left hand, my fingers seem to burn off. I bite my tongue to prevent myself from screaming out. Cradling my hand, I open the freezer with my shoulder and plunge my arm inside up to the elbow, between a packet of frozen peas and two bottles of vodka, until the throbbing subsides and my fingers grow numb.

A noise from the hall distracts me from concentrating on the numbness creeping up my arm. I pull it out of the freezer and close the door, stepping towards the archway to watch *le gosse* peeling himself out of the blanket and warily eyeing me. His hair has dried to a mop of tousled brown mass, and he is chewing on his lower lip. I remember the glass of milk and glancing behind me, I locate a box of cereal on the middle shelf, which I pull out and place on the table. Then I march briskly through the hall, careful not to make eye contact. I can feel him watching me, and as I reach the stairs, I hear him slide into the kitchen. Mounting the stairs, I try to push his presence out of my mind.

The water coming out of the shower is only lukewarm, because I have not switched on the boiler. It is in the cupboard next to John's study, to which the door is half open, inviting, sending out little wafts of bookish air and printed paper and loose tobacco. I tend to rush past the door on the little landing, not breathing, looking strictly ahead.

I have finished dressing in several layers of woollen jumpers and long johns under my pants, readying myself to go for a walk along the coast, when the telephone rings. I freeze with my hands in the air, ready to wrap my scarf around my head. When it rings again, I let the scarf trail behind me as I slowly walk down to the hall, where the telephone rings as if anybody was actually calling here. I stop a few steps in front of the table. *Le gosse* stands on the other side, looking petrified. The phone rings again, and he jerks his head up to me as I move towards it. His hair has lifted away from his eyes, he's sporting a shiner. As I reach the table, the phone rings again, and for a split second I think he will sweep it to the floor before I can pick it up.

'Hello?' I say into the heavy black receiver, and *le gosse* clamps both his hands around the edge of the table, the left half of his lower lip firmly caught between his teeth. I suddenly realise I can't remember his name.

'Henry,' I greet my brother-in-law. My unwanted houseguest seems to swoon. He stares at me imploringly and starts shaking his head. I listen to Henry and watch his son, who has gone completely still, drained of all colour, clinging onto the table for dear life. I raise my eyebrows at him, and he forms a silent 'no' with his mouth. I remember Henry's cold hands and his cufflinks, and how he would not talk to me, directing his questions at John, even when they concerned me, even after I had long learned the language.

'Why would he come here?' I ask, breaking eye contact with *le gosse*, whose arm shoots forward to hit down on the cradle. I snap my head back to him and give him a warning look, and he keeps his trembling hand hovering over the cradle, not daring to touch it.

'John's gone,' I say into the phone. 'You know it, I know it, I assume your *gamins* know it as well.'

Le gosse is holding his breath, and I feel myself almost being pushed over the edge by Henry, who seems to have forgotten why he initially called and tries to bring up the subject of John again.

I cut him short.

'I don't have time for this. He's… I'll believe he's dead when I see it. Should your son turn up here, I'll let you know.' It's a warning to *le gosse* to stay out of my way, and I can see him getting the message. He backs away from the phone and resumes breathing, sitting down on the kitchen doorstep. I hang up and move to the coat rack to put on my oilskin. My old zip-up sweater falls to the floor. I pick it up, then throw it to him.

'Heating's unreliable,' I say, and leave through the front door. The wet air is breathtaking.

When I come down the stairs the next morning, *le gosse* is again sleeping on the old sofa in the hall. He has found one of the embroidered pillows that I had pushed against the loose skirting boards to keep the draught out, and my oilskin is folded neatly on top of the black trunk.

I stop on the last step, my hand clenched around the banister, my left foot rubbing against my right shin. It's cold in the hall, there's a draught coming from the far end, where the French windows open into the garden. From the stained glass window over the front door, red and green light falls onto the slates, and the door to the kitchen is wide open, so it is light enough to see that the kid has broken the phone. The pieces are sorted on the round telephone table, the shattered receiver lying delicately on its side, the cable unplugged and rolled up tightly.

I hesitantly take a step off the stairs, directly onto the Persian carpet that will allow me to walk barefoot over to the telephone table. I walk on tip-toes past the sofa, where *le gosse* lies wrapped up tightly, and invisible but for the hair, which looks wet again, as if he's just come in from the rain. Maybe he has. The other night, he probably rang the doorbell out of respect. The nephew I remember knows how to pick locks and how to enter houses through kitchen windows.

I stand in front of the telephone table and look down at the broken phone, at the neat row of tiny screws and nuts, arranged in size. He must have hurled it across the room to achieve that level of damage. There's a folded piece of paper as well, held down by the earpiece. I slid it out from under the black plastic and flip it open. It contains a banknote and a single word written on the paper: 'Sorry'. *Le gosse*'s handwriting eerily reminds me of John. I unfold the banknote just as I hear him sit up behind me. I look over my shoulder, and he stares back, attentively.

I don't care about the phone. I haven't touched it in days until yesterday, so I'm not even angry. But now I am holding a bank note in my hand I've only ever seen in pictures before, the value is so high.

'Is this supposed to cover the rent as well?' I ask.

Le gosse cocks his head.

'Could it?' he asks. His voice is hoarse.

I shrug, let the note fall back on the table and go to the coat rack to step into my wellies. I know I should ask him where he got it, but I can't be bothered. I have to go and stare at the sea to will the boat back home.

The sea hits lazily against the granite rocks, which are covered in seaweed coughed up during the storm, and the water is muddy and brown with all the dirt it dug up from the ground. I climb up the rocks to the one closest to the shore and protruding furthest towards the horizon. I tie the belt of my coat faster, turn up the collar and sit down. The sea rumbles in a disgruntled manner, and I give it the finger. Then I wrap my hands up in the folds of my scarf.

I have not heard him coming, but suddenly, *le gosse* is standing next to me, holding out my thermos. He's wearing my old oilskin, which comes down to below his knees, and a woollen hat which I recognise as John's.

'Take it off,' I say.

'It's Uncle John's,' he answers, as if that meant he's entitled to wear it. He's still holding out the thermos, and there is a stubborn look on his face which must be hereditary.

'*Ne me fait pas chier*, take it off,' I repeat, ignoring the thermos.

'It's fucking freezing,' he replies, placing the thermos at my feet and backing away before I can snatch the hat from his head.

It's the insolence which throws me, the blatant disregard for manners which is so familiar to me, and before I can stop myself, I give in to the curiosity which has awoken two nights ago and which has grown ever since.

'Why are you here?'

Le gosse shifts uneasily but seems to decide that he owes me an answer.

'I need a place to stay.'

'You've got a place to stay.'

His voice is very small when he says, 'I can't be there right now.'

He's clearly uncomfortable, but then he's wearing John's hat, and that comes at a high price, so I'm prodding further.

'Why did you come here?'

He looks me straight in the eye when he says: 'Because you won't care whether I'm here or not.'

This is a bit unsettling to me. I pick up the thermos and screw it open to smell the content. Tea. Quite a good tea, as far as I can tell, which means...

'You searched through the cupboards.'

He admits it nodding, stepping from foot to foot to keep warm, and I pour some of the tea into the cup and hold it out to him. He looks so small in my oilskin. He takes the cup in both hands, his fingers only just sticking out of the sleeves, and I can see he has bitten down the nails of almost all his fingers. I turn away from him and stare over the sea.

'What are you looking at?' he asks, following my gaze.

'*La mer,*' I say.

'You've looked at it all morning,' he says, 'is there anything interesting to see?'

'It's hiding something,' I answer, '*va-t'en*.'

He doesn't. He crouches down on a rock not far from me and searches the horizon with his eyes, a deep crease forming between his brows.

'Are you waiting for a boat?' he asks, and I find myself thinking that he is playing with me, *le gosse*, he knows what I am looking for, everybody knows that, the whole family has probably been talking about my follies for months. I turn towards him and give him an angry look, and he buries his face in the steam coming up from the cup. I decide to push him further now, he cannot ask me these questions and think I won't do the same to him.

'How did you come here?'

He lets the cup fall, and when he scrambles up to run away, I jump up and catch him by the collar of my oilskin. The garment is so big that he can squirm his way out of the sleeves and duck into it, emerging underneath the hem, but then he stumbles over the rocks, and he would have fallen on his face if I was not grabbing him around the chest. He trembles like a wild thing. I heave him to his feet and turn him around, facing me.

'How?'

'Lorry' he whispers, and I let him go. He wraps his arms around himself, I realise it has started to drizzle, and I pick up the oilskin from the ground and shove it at him.

With a lorry. He must have crawled under the planes at a checkpoint, in the middle of the night when the controls are laxer, and he can only have got until the border with it. There is no way he could have been smuggled over the canal in a lorry: every vehicle is literally taken apart before they are allowed to cross. He can see me working through this and shrugs.

'I swam.'

'Through the canal?'

'Yes.'

It's disconcerting, I think, and it is more than I wanted to know. He could have died.

'I only need a place to stay,' he says, and he looks as if he might cry. I take a step back and pick up the thermos to walk back towards the house. He follows me; I can hear him jumping from rock to rock. He could slip and fall, I think, and my concern surprises me.

When I reach the door, he squeezes through it under my arm and vanishes into the back of the hall, where I hear him rustling with the oilskin and sneezing.

'What is it, your name?' I ask, and he stills. I wonder whether he had preferred it when I didn't want to know.

'Kip,' he finally says, his voice wavering thin and small through the semi-darkness.

'Really,' I say. I don't remember his name, but I know it's not Kip. I am annoyed with him, he has taken up much of my time, so I turn and climb up the stairs.

'Samuel,' he calls, 'it's Samuel. But mostly it's Kip.'

I stop and look down, he stands in the middle of the hall, his eyes as big as saucers.

'You should probably take a bath,' I say, pointing at the bathroom door at the top of the stairs. Then I remember the boiler, and I freeze.

Kip has followed me up the stairs and looks at me questioningly.

'There's no hot water,' I say.

He can see I'm lying. I take the next step and stop again.

'The boiler needs to be switched on.' I almost choke on the words, and I pull myself upwards one more step, until I am on the landing, where I sit down on the floor. Kip crouches down next to me.

'Marie,' he says, and I wonder how he remembered me, he has only met me once, he must have prepared this trip very well, 'Marie, are you sick?'

I shake my head, I start to cry, and John's nephew sits back on his haunches, at a loss, I try to find my voice, I cannot lose my composure now, not now that I have almost forced *la tempête* to give me my treasure back.

'Cupboard,' I manage, 'the boiler is in the cupboard.'

Kip stands up and opens the brown double doors to reveal the dusty green boiler. He looks back to me over his shoulder, I point towards the switch at the top right. He can reach it when he rises on his toes. He comes back to me and sits down again.

'Can I stay here until the borders are fully closed?' he asks.

I nod.

GLORIA
DAWSON

LAPSE

Maybe I could remove this coat
of imagining our funerals. The river of marble
outside the Grand Hotel is wet as coal
softening soles, helping the feet forget.

Walking on in the morning
with the thought folded over my arm,
taking steps from it.

All languages are spoken here, which in the lobby blend
to none; only the sing of pulse, the tinnitus
of an approaching plane or seconds leaving.

Damascus, box-carving and beautiful idea, through you
I am carrying news of our deaths, which on that plane
are always eloquent, and perfectly translated.

A LA FIN TU ES LAS

The golden trinity of pawnbrokers is hanging posed
over the slow
                    traffic of the Walworth Road
        dark
underground, too, and in the light—the worst kind
and the two black girls
                            arguing over last night's lusts
                in pink
and the woman who wears   pink   Chanel sunglasses but takes the bus
so that we can see them   sunlight is the nearest gold to God this morning
and we'll glimpse them   mining dreams and blinding doorways
minion of the drunk the sick the old
you pass too fast to give
more meaning but

today you may withdraw—
indefinitely grinding round the roundabout at Elephant
and the rattle of the unstruck Underground

And so—the engine is turning a thousand-time waltz
of powerful horses with petrolly tails
which spill on the asphalt and spread in the rain
into rainbows and fractals unbearably hard
to bear your love   dies on Wednesday and is risen again for Friday night

his body's far   but not here
these shops used   find it there
these not used

domine dirige nos   A Smile Costs Nothing!
at the pawnbrokers   Thrift Is Blessing
                    today you may withdraw
ALL THE COATS
IN THE SALE
ARE HALF PRICE
TILL NEXT WEEK

and there are cloaks
white cloaks on the women, unknowing penitents and knowing sinners
doing the washing up and singing foreign songs

BENJAMIN MORRIS

WHAT I LIKE IN FIGHTS

Petals flying through the air;
shards of glass upon the floor;
the fear that it will never end;
the knowing there are always more

edges waiting in your voice,
the chances given like a gift
to find them all, to tease them out,
to slice my mind upon their kiss;

remembering that words are sharp
as the very idea of a razor;
the sudden outbreak of a laugh
as a fire leaps into a blaze, or

a hand condenses into a fist.
All this and more I love, my love,
but none so much as you, the you
for whom enough is not enough.

THE APRICOT PIT

But when I drop it,
and it clatters to the sidewalk,
nestling between the cracks
between one massive plate

and another, what they did *not*
tell me at the fruit stand
was that it would take root
in the stone, and ripple

underneath my feet as I stand
there savouring its flesh; or that
by the time I have swallowed
leafbuds would have freckled

the slender stalk now
pushing itself up like a swimmer
through the dark undulations
of gravity and of air,

or that branches would be
sparking off like neurons
toward the rapidly assembling
crowd; or that, after

I have finished the final apricot
in my rustling market bag,
and the tree that looms over
the street has begun dropping

fruit like a heavy cloud
sloughs off its laden rain,
we all pause, and look on it
for a moment, collect a few

for a pocket home, then
turn back to our former thoughts,
step over the quivering roots,
and begin to sing?

HITCHIN

We only knew it as a town
to pass through, its little name
and little worlds sliding past us
on the train: its drinkards,
its cuckolds, its cats. If we had
stopped there, for no reason at all,
would we have found a corner
where you suddenly propose,
two names colliding above our heads?

On the far hill a white horse stands
sentinel against this melody,
shuttered against the window
we had built to admit it,
and so I ask: come, O hills,
form your congress to crush
this town of glass and salt and smoke.
Come, O sky, reclaim what is yours,
what these buildings have stolen

from you and hidden away.
Come, O soil, open your mouth
and slake the thirst you have harboured
since the first brick was laid,
so that what is left of our sweat
upon the earth will rise up and vanish,
will find new ways to be forgotten,
the old ones leaving our hands
stained red with rust.

JASON
MORTON

THE BASICS OF TIME TRAVEL

College kids just moved in across the street; now they're having a party. I can see them smoking by the front door, the girls in short skirts, cold autumn air, I can see how they want to be fucked. Play with them first, make like you love them; breathe heavier when you're near the ear.

I sit in my window and think about fucking eighteen-year-olds for a good five minutes. Till the cigarette's dead. These kids ain't thinking about work, any of it. They wanna drink, chat, flirt and fuck, in no particular order. And there's no law against it.

So I walk to the kitchen, grab a half a fifth of whiskey and lock up on the way out. I do my best to not make a beeline for their front door. There's people filling the lawn, though, and I put a cigarette in my mouth. I even go so far as to fake looking for a lighter.

I approach a girl with blond hair over black, a black-and-white striped shirt making her look maybe a little thicker than she actually is. 'Hey babe, gotta light?'

She's got friends around but smiles, handing me the lighter with her pinky slightly raised. I like that. It's a cheap one and it just chik-chiks when I try to light it.

'Need a hand with that thing?' she asks.

'Maybe.'

'Here... It needs the magic touch.'

She gets the flame going and I light up with my head cocked to the side; I can see her looking on from the corner of my eye.

She says, 'Where ya headed with that bottle?'

'Don't know,' I say. 'What's shakin' here?'

She mentions some names that I forget as soon as I hear them. She says I should stick around, if I want. I do and we chat about movies and college, music and college, her parents, her classes and college. And am I in college? I think to play the part for a minute, but quickly decide I'm not that good a liar. Girl seems pretty quick, she'd probably know, so I tell her I been done with that scene for a while now. She keeps talkin' like that don't matter. And that bottle of mine keeps getting lower. And lower. She kisses me on the cheek and says, 'I gotta piss.'

God, I love them classy broads.

She's gone, and now some weaselly-looking little shit asks me for a light, and I think, Yeah, why not another? So we ask around and find one. And he's a pretty funny kid, moved up from Chicago, and we end up chatting for quite a while.

And the party dies all around us without us really noticing. When I go inside to piss and hopefully steal a beer or two, there's a few people in the kitchen (how do the stragglers always end up in the kitchen?) and bodies passed out in the kind of humidity that only comes from a party with too many people.

I talk to the stragglers for a minute, while a girl at the table peels the label off a half-finished MGD. Looks like she's peeled one too many. One of the guys has a half-hour slot on the local 'alternative' radio station. The other guy's older brother went to my high school, starting four years after I finished. This one's a freshman at the university now, and try as I might, I don't give a shit. I make a quick break for the bathroom and drain into the toilet, getting that shake that always comes with a real good piss, the slight leg twitch, just wondering when it's gonna end, and come back out — fuck washing hands at this hour.

The fridge is all condiments and milk. A dozen cans of Coke, give or take. And who keeps a damn cantaloupe in the fridge? But more importantly, no beer. I can see why this crowd thinned out. The girl's still peeling the label off the MGD, the fluid level still the same, when I ask, 'You done with this?'

I barely wait for a reply before taking it and draining it, washing away that whiskey and stale smoke taste with the lukewarm beer. Nod at the stragglers on the way out of the kitchen.

The living room looks like a damn battlefield, kids laid out on everything that won't move, chairs, couches, a table, the floor. And I see the blond-over-black cozied up next to some punk more her age, at least the right decade. They're both asleep and she looks as good as ever with her eyes shut, the arm he's wrapped around her pushing up her breasts. I walk over closer, thinking that maybe I could wake her up and get her over to my place with the promise of a clean bed. I think better of it by the time I get there, but I'm not sober enough to talk myself outta giving her a quick kiss on the forehead before I go, giving me a sweet second to smell the flower scent in her hair.

The boy wakes up for a moment, looks me in the eyes. He might've been pissed for all I know, but I take my head back slowly just the same. 'I'm her uncle,' I say, returning to the spent-liquor atmosphere, and his eyes close.

The weaselly shit's still standing on the lawn when I walk out.

'Fuck, man,' he says, 'Where'd everybody go?'

I keep on walking. 'Home.'

KAPKA
KASSABOVA

BUENOS AIRES: WHEN I RETURN

Said the taxi driver

'You're Bulgarian, you moved to New Zealand, and now you live in Scotland,' said the taxi driver and studied me in the front mirror. 'Couldn't you come up with a more weird combination?'

'I do my best,' I said.

'Whereas I was born in Buenos Aires, I've lived in Buenos Aires all my life, and I will die in Buenos Aires. This is what my epitaph will say. The biography of an ordinary *porteño*. With no ambitions to go anywhere. Not because I'm all that happy here, but because I'll be even unhappier away from here.

'This country is colonised, culturally,' said the taxi driver, 'Nothing is ours. In the 30s and 40s, we wanted to be like France. Then like England. In the 70s came American culture. Now, we just don't know what the hell we are. Nothing we have is ours.'

'Except tango.'

'Except tango.'

'And maté.'

'Yes, maté as well.'

'And the *lunfardo* slang of Buenos Aires.'

'That's true.'

'Foreigners love coming here.'

'It's not a bad country, really. I'm personally quite fond of it. No, I wouldn't change it for the world!'

Hotel Astoria

It was 2001, the country was in meltdown, and Jason and I seemed to be the only guests of the Hotel Astoria. The *cazerolazos* had frightened tourists away. But one afternoon, I met another hotel guest in the lift. He was a man with a trimmed grey beard, standing stiffly in an impeccable pinstriped suit. He pointed a prosthetic hand at me:

'Ah, you speak English!' he said in mannered English, 'You can be my chauffeur when I become president. In twenty days, I shall be president of this country.'

'This country seems to need a new president indeed,' I said in my best received pronunciation — I didn't want to let him down.

'Yes,' he nodded solemnly, 'Look me up in twenty days.' He handed me a campaign leaflet with a blurry photograph. I could make no sense of the text. When I asked the receptionist later, he tapped his forehead and said 'The gentleman is not all there.'

We weren't all there either. For a month, Jason and I stayed in the Hotel Astoria, one of the many Romantic buildings along the Avenida de Mayo with lace-like façades. Our balcony looked out onto the once grand avenue. At the top, cupolas with shattered windows gaped darkly like extinguished eyes. At the bottom, the city acted out its theatre of rage. Leaning over the wrought-iron railing, we watched each night's demonstrations like mute envoys from some state without a name.

We watched the collapse with a mix of morbid fascination and real fear that this was the end of Buenos Aires as the world knew it. Down in the wrecked, littered street, a giant orange penis on wheels was being pushed by protesters, with a sign that said 'Pesification your balls.' The usual banging of pots and pans accompanied the procession. We flicked the TV channels. There was a carnival on which merged with the carnivalesque protest marches. A clown with a permanent grin said to the camera: 'I'm happy. I don't know what people are complaining about. I don't have any problems, I just want to laugh.' A woman dressed as a ragged Justice, blindfolded and holding a balance, staggered around bloodied and violated. 'The Carnival is on,' said breathlessly a dancing acrobat, 'the government says it's not but we want our right to be joyful. Joy is the only thing they haven't robbed us of.'

On the 'models' channel, nubile girls crawled along beaches pouting inanely at the camera while greasy men with toupees 'interviewed' them. 'I'm deeply Catholic,' said one young thing with a large crucifix over her pubescent chest. 'Actually, I'm fanatical.'

On the non-stop tango channel, it was business as usual. '*Queridos amigos del tango*,' the programme host smiled, showing his artificial teeth. For hours on end, prostrate like heavily drugged patients in a two-person asylum, we watched, transfixed, the televised feet of tango dancers.

We went on a pilgrimage to San Telmo, the semi-restored *barrio* near the Port Madero. The *conventillo* houses, once mansions for rich families, were now peeling and their plastered balconies were falling off. In the dingy doorways I glimpsed the kind of dingy life hopeful immigrants had lived and continued to live. The only difference was where they came from — once they were European, now they were South American. Once they had been welcome, now they weren't.

In Plaza Dorrego, a couple were dancing tango for the few tourists — business as usual. I recognised Leo, the melodramatic tango clown with black, Chaplin-esque eyebrows and smart waistcoat. He had been dancing here the previous year too. After a few sets with his black-and-red painted girl, he pulled out a woman from the audience. She turned out to be a tango professional. She was painfully thin, wore shorts and a T-shirt, and had a tragic, ghostly face with a red mouth. Fidgety and un-happy, she danced like a paper ballerina in some cold draft of the soul.

'Shit,' Jason said, 'that's Dolores. Looking very thin.'

Dolores was his ex. He didn't want to step out and greet her, not with me around. Instead, he met her for coffee that week, and came back de-pressed. The meeting had ended with bitter recriminations.

'She's bitter about everything, about living here, about being Argentine, about me, about men in general. It's like life hasn't delivered for her. But what has she done to deserve more? I fell for her because of her veneer. She had glamour and sophistication, and I mistook that for depth.'

How convenient that we have a blind spot for the inevitable. Another year and a half would go by until Jason would apologise that he had fallen for my 'veneer' of immigration and displacement, only to fall out with the real person I turned out to be.

But already, the process was underway. Jason sat in the *milongas*, washed up on these shores like a wet log that had floated for too long in indifferent oceans. He rarely danced, saying he was out of form. Instead, he gazed into the dance floor, seized by some unfathomable heart-sickness. It was as if the present, even in Buenos Aires, even at the heart of the tango world, simply couldn't deliver.

One night, after hours of sitting with him in a depressed catatonia and not getting invited by other men because I was accompanied, I cracked. On the way back in the taxi, I told Jason that he was crushing my spirit. He said that he resented being responsible for my happiness. I said that he should be more worried about his own happiness. He said that's the way he was and if I didn't like it...

'Where are you from?' the taxi driver interrupted in Spanish and turned down the music on the 24-hour tango station.

'New Zealand,' I said grumpily.

'Is it easy to emigrate to New Zealand?'

This was only the tenth time a taxi driver had mentioned emigrating. As our own romantic misery evolved, we became increasingly incapable of dealing with other people's misery. Back in the Hotel Astoria, it was impossible to be in the same room together, so I stormed out into the small dark hours. I started walking in the deserted streets, blinded by that helpless feeling which we mistake for anger but which is a precursor to grief.

Outside, the *cartoneros* were picking out cartons and other treasures from the rubbish containers. They shouted hello cheerfully. Further on, another group of men loading stuff onto a truck shouted obscenities, and I turned into a darker side street. It'll serve him right if I get raped, I thought. There, among the gutted rubbish and dug-out pavement stones, I sat down in a recessed window and cried out what felt like my entire heart's contents.

Somewhere in the recesses of another time, muffled but unmistakable, was playing the constant music of loss, heartbreak and disappointment. Like the tango TV channel, it played non-stop. And now that I could suddenly tune into it, I was stuck with it. I didn't know whether it was the past or the future that this music trickled from, whether it was a premonition of my own future or a reaction to my past, but either way everything seemed hopeless. Buenos Aires was not the city it had been, and neither was this new love. Everything slipped into disrepair sooner or later. No golden era, no honeymoon lasted forever. Erosion was inevitable, and tango expressed this with perfect, masochistic precision.

After a long time of feeling sorry for Argentina and for myself, during which I secretly hoped Jason would appear and save the night, a man came out of the doorway where I was sitting. A red light shone on the inside. I looked at the sign above the door. It was a pornographic video joint.

'You okay, pretty?' the man said. He was holding a couple of videos. He was middle-aged and had worn-out cowboy boots. He looked let down by life. 'Are you waiting for someone?'

'No,' I said. 'Because he's not going to come.'

'Then he's not worth waiting for.' He turned to go, then stopped and concluded over his shoulder, 'Nothing's worth waiting for, if you ask me. Nothing and nobody.'

He melted into the night. Eventually, I took his advice and melted into the night too. Buenos Aires had absorbed so much heartbreak over the last century that one more person hardly mattered.

Meanwhile, we have tango

I met Carlos one night in the Porteño y Bailarin salon where Jason and I took classes. He had a ponytail, looked unkempt, and danced differently from the other Argentine men. 'No, I'm not a foreigner,' Carlos said, 'I'm a local. Although I live in Brazil now. People often mistake me for a foreigner, I don't know why. But I'm not sensitive about these things — German, Swiss, whatever makes you happy.'

His Brazilian wife was there too, looking miserable when he danced with other women, which he kept to a minimum, 'to keep the peace.'

'It's impossible to have a good time when you're with your partner. You have to go dancing alone,' he whispered to me confidentially.

I glanced at Jason who was looking his usual wretched self at our table, and agreed. Next time I saw Carlos at Club Canning, I was upset after another clash with Jason in the hotel. Carlos was there on his own too — his wife had gone back to Brazil.

'It's difficult for her, and I can't relax when she's around. But why this face? I can see your man's back from Brazil.' Jason had gone to Brazil the previous week, for a friend's wedding.

I was smoking the last of my cigarillos and teetering, with my shaky high heels, on the verge of nervous collapse — in other words, I was being a tango caricature. Carlos was kind enough not to point this out.

'I'll have your cigarillo box. My wife collects boxes. I want to keep the peace. But anyway, you know this won't last forever. You won't be in love forever. The good times will come back. I know about these things, my wife is a psychologist. Seriously. Meanwhile, we have tango, thank god, or rather thanks to Pugliese. God has never done anything for me, but just listen to Pugliese!'

Carlos danced me into temporary happiness. Tango made us all happy because it was a flattering distillation of our lives. It was the highlights without the daily grind. It was the promise without the flawed delivery. It was the seduction without the disappointment. The night of passion without the morning after. The yearning without the madness. The angst without the suicide. I stayed in touch with Carlos. The following year, I split up with Jason, and Carlos split up with his wife and moved back to Buenos Aires.

'I felt bad in Brazil, like a rat leaving the sinking ship,' he wrote, 'Now

I know that this is my place in the world, and I will stay here until the end.'

I envied him for having a place in the world at all.

San Telmo tango sanatorium

Back in Buenos Aires four years later, I walked around San Telmo. A dog-walker with stubble and a baseball cap pulled along seven large dogs. The shops were closing down for the afternoon. The buildings were peeling as ever, and graffiti sprawled across the walls: VIAJEROS, BAJOS FONDOS, LOS TOXICOS, LOS NEUROTICOS ANONIMOS. I wasn't sure if these were musical bands or states of mind.

I went to take an afternoon tango class in Confitería Ideal, the tango institution where everything is frozen in some cobwebbed *belle époque*: the cakes, the fans, the gorgeous chandeliers, the waiters in waistcoats. Even the people who came here to dance seemed to have a dated air, like forgotten extras in a Fellini movie.

Next, I went in search of tango shoes. In one shop, a young woman with woolly black hair kept confusing the shop assistant with her rudimentary Spanish, and then turning her away to fetch more shoes, like a princess tired of her stupid servants. She was Russian, from Boston.

'I want a shoe that doesn't exist,' she turned to me. 'I want to design it and have it custom-made. She doesn't understand that.'

Embarrassed on behalf of all arrogant foreigners, I sat in a café, drank killer coffee, and watched two middle-aged identical twins dressed and moustachioed as Charlie Chaplin. They made rubbery, puzzled faces at me. I asked them whether they were actors.

'We are, when somebody needs us to be,' one answered cryptically.

'Where do you act?' I insisted.

'Wherever we are called to act,' the other said.

When I left, they tipped their bowler hats off to me.

Back at my San Telmo tenement, flu was going round the hotel. The place resembled a run-down sanatorium for tubercular patients with tango delusions. A prisoner of my grim bed, I lay under the drumming of rain on the plastic bathroom roof, watched the moody skies of spring through the high window, and listened to the noises of the hotel. A muddle of languages echoed along the patio, and from the dance room came the sounds of tango and coughing: somebody was always practicing there, night and day, in sickness and in health.

I got to know the other patients. Zoraida was the receptionist and general person-about-the-place. She lived here, moving from one empty room to another, following the comings and goings of guests. Zoraida was voluptuous, sharp-tongued and moody. She offered cheap tango classes to guests of the hotel, and despite her size, danced like a nymph. She could be found reclining on the kitchen bench like a concubine in some derelict harem. She was always snacking on fatty foods and holding forth on whatever subject was at hand, in Spanish or in English. I asked her how often she went dancing.

'As often as possible. I'm chronically under-slept. I'm a tango zombie. I love it. Tango is not about steps and sequences, you know. It's about connecting. When dancing personalities connect, that's when the magic happens. And when they don't connect at all, it's crap. That's why you can never get bored with tango. Because you never know what you might experience.

'You know, I spent two years living in Los Angeles and Brazil. And I decided to come back. I was missing tango. I was missing the people, the cafés, the culture — look at how much is happening here. Rio doesn't have that. Los Angeles is a graveyard, everybody at home, nobody in the streets. So I came back. But when the elections were on during the crisis, and that son of a bitch Menem was going to run for elections again, after all he'd done to the country, I said to my mother: if he wins, I'm gonna immolate myself, like a Muslim woman. If the rest of Argentina can live with this, I can't. Thank god he pulled out, so I didn't have to die for my country. But things are going better now. This government is the best we've had in ages. It's a good time for Argentina.'

With us in the kitchen was a placid Swiss guy in his late twenties called

Pekka. He was waiting for a Dutch girl with whom he practiced. He was thin and dry, with furtive fish eyes. He was living here, learning tango and writing his thesis on 'the economics of tango.' He spoke a slow, methodical English, like an electronic voice dictionary.

'How much longer will you stay here?' I asked.

'As long as it is necessary. I want to be able to speak to Argentines, and to connect with dancers. I want to be a good tango dancer. Maybe I will stay for four more months, maybe more. It depends if something happens.'

'Like what? Falling in love at a *milonga*?' I teased.

'I do not think this will happen.'

No, I didn't think so either. Later, I saw him in a *milonga*. He danced the same way as he spoke — correct, expressionless, frosty, his face a blond mask of hard work and quiet confidence. Not quite a tango Nazi, but a tango clerk — taking diligent notes, filing them away, dangling the keys to the secret offices of tango without any wonder or emotion. Or maybe I misread him completely in the Argentine context of wearing your heart on your sleeve. Maybe underneath the android façade there was a hot inferno of Swiss passion.

The Dutch girl Lara he practiced with had a blunt, garrulous personality, like a cheerful tractor. She danced from morning to morning, often practicing by herself in the dance room. She bought endless pairs of tango shoes for her handsome, large Dutch feet. She wanted to be a tango teacher in Amsterdam. In her eyes lived the spark of tango folly. There, I saw glorious, sweeping moves, an admiring audience, a following of pupils, the name Lara in large letters on posters, her own website, travelling Europe as a tango teacher, perhaps even an escape from her boring job in PR. When I said I couldn't afford to buy more than one pair of shoes, she looked surprised and asked what I did for a living. What crappy job could be so low-paid as to make such a trifling thing as a pair of shoes in a third-world country too expensive?

'Writer! That's great! You can write about tango,' she offered, and then paused to think. 'I do not read anymore. I used to read until my exams but then I stopped reading. I have no time to read. My life is work, tango, sleep, work, tango, sleep.'

'When were your exams?'

'When I was eighteen.'

She was now 31. In the kitchen, regardless of the audience, she expressed every thought she had.

'I have had a wonderful time here for a few days, dancing a lot,' she said while making herself a sensible breakfast of muesli and yoghurt. 'But last night, this man asked me out. I did not know what to say. I do not want to offend him because he is a good dancer and I want to dance with him again.' She turned to me. 'Have you been here on your own before?'

'This is my first time completely alone,' I said.

But she had already moved on to the next subject.

'I do not think I need another cup of tea, because the water will be in my stomach, making noises when I dance.'

'I didn't need that image,' said Tim, the New Zealander. 'Can you take it back please?'

Tim was the in-house whinger. He was long and dangly, with a caved-in chest, as if someone had accidentally unplugged his will to live. He had the eyes of a sensitive toad. Like the rest of him, his eyes always glided to your side when he talked to you. When he spoke, his head quivered atop his long thin neck like some sick vegetable, possibly a turnip. Like the ruddy, brash in-house Australian Rod, he wore the antipodean uniform of hiking boots, rain-jacket, moleskin trousers and fleece jumpers — ideal for the Australian outback or the isolated farm where Tim lived, but incongruous in Buenos Aires, and simply grotesque in the world of tango. Seeing that both Lara and I were coughing, Tim said helpfully:

'I had this flu at the beginning, a month ago. I was so pleased I wasn't just staying for two weeks and wasting my time.'

He knew that both of us were staying for two weeks. When I mentioned that I was going to a clinic, Tim said:

'I hope you're not going to the hospital! In my first week, I had a spot of diarrhoea, and I went to the hospital. I had to wait for two hours, and then I realised the labs were closed for the weekend. It was hell.'

'This city is falling to pieces, have you seen it?' Tim went on. 'I don't know why they don't fix it. There are bricks falling off the roofs, they can kill you. I try to walk under construction shelters, to protect myself. And the holes in the pavement, have you seen them? I don't know why they don't fix them.'

'When you're feeling better, I'd like to practice my backward *ochos* with you,' he said once.

'Sure,' I lied. This is why I had come to Buenos Aires — to practice my *ochos* with the Grim Reaper while he tells me about his diarrhoea. I saw him in a *milonga* the following week: with funereal oblivion to the music, he roughly manoeuvred his victim into backward *ochos*. Zoraida gave him a lesson in the practice room.

'Really,' she fumed later, 'I don't know what is wrong with these people — Australians, New Zealanders, English, Canadians, they always have problems. These Anglo Saxons are the worst, always unhappy.'

A new patient arrived one day: she was hairy-faced, nervy, and spoke an intelligent English. I assumed she was German, but she turned out to be from Norway. A couple of days later, relaxed in the knowledge that I too had mixed allegiances, she revealed her guilty secret: she was, after all, German.

'Sometimes I say I'm from Germany, sometimes Norway. The reactions are very different. It's much easier to be from Norway. Nobody cares about Norway. But being German, you carry around all the baggage of the war. And the image of being over-organised. But I don't know what I am anymore, to tell the truth. In Germany, I feel alien. I always did, that's why I left ten years ago. In Norway, I'm a German, and always will be.'

At *milongas*, she sat alone, drank red wine, and was over the moon whenever someone invited her to dance. She was the only person in our hotel who was nice to Tim, though she drew the line at dancing with him. Watching her at the *milongas*, always alone and always smiling, practically invisible in her plainness and modesty among the glammed-up, pouting tango princess, I wondered if tango was her only outlet, her only lover.

The Dutch woman emerged from her fever. Still coughing and feeble, she threw herself back into her punishing tango regime.

'I had a nightmare,' she said in the kitchen in between coughing fits. 'I was dreaming that I am dancing, and trying to do a step, and I cannot, it is not working. I wanted to stop, I said to myself, you have to stop, you are tired. But I couldn't, I kept dancing badly, I was so tired and ashamed of my bad dancing, and I just wanted to lie down. But I couldn't stop dancing.'

The Australians, the Turks, the Argentine, the Norwegian German, the Bulgarian Kiwi — we all smiled at her earnest obsession. But we were smiling out of embarrassment. Because in the tango sanatorium of San Telmo, in our crepuscular rooms full of damp shoes, we had all had that fevered nightmare.

The eternal *milonguita*

'Can you live from music lessons?'

'Well, you can see for yourself.' Carlos swept an arm over his joyless bachelor's studio flat furnished with the brownest, saddest of furniture. 'This is how I live.'

This was the first time I had seen Carlos in the daylight, outside a *milonga*. He seemed older and balder. Perhaps we all seemed older, if not balder, away from the dim lights of the tango salons. His eyes seemed tired, despite the quick laughter his face was used to. His intelligent, dynamic head clashed with the drabness of his abode. There was no kitchen, only a cupboard and a fridge. A single bed, a couch, a computer station and a wall full of disks. The view from the only window was of a deep, narrow courtyard, a kind of lightless well, although we were on the ninth floor. We sat at the small table and drank maté.

'You know, at tango, I keep a very low profile. A girl I know told me the other day, 'You keep an obscenely low profile. And the weird thing about you is, you really are like that. It's not a façade, you really don't care about things.' I said to her, what things am I supposed to care about?

But you know, Argentine women still have a third-world mentality, very conservative. Family values, a breadwinner husband, little kiddies, and that's it. It's hopeless.'

'But surely there are independent, educated women out there too...'

'Show them to me! I want to see them.'

I couldn't. I didn't know any.

'Anyway, that's why I say that tango is a product of crisis. Crisis of identity — not the identity of the nation anymore, but the identity of masculinity and femininity, of how the sexes relate. That's why it's still a dance of the margins. The lawyers, doctors and bankers who dance tango often hide it from their colleagues. Because for those who dance tango, something is missing.'

'But what about couples? Couples dance too,' I protested, and immediately saw the idiocy of my remark. We looked at each other and laughed, recalling our unhappy exes.

'Exactly,' he said gleefully, 'The couple amplifies. If one or both people are happy, the couple is fantastic. If both are unhappy, it's hell. And tango amplifies this happiness or unhappiness.'

'Even if one is unhappy that's enough,' I said, thinking of Jason at his wretched table and Carlos' jealous Brazilian wife in that distant *milonga* of the past.

'That's plenty,' he said. 'But sometimes, people go dancing only to find a lover. Once they settle in a relationship, they quit dancing. Then there are those who confuse things. This Mexican-American woman wanted me to have sex with her after our lessons. I said, no but thanks anyway. You can pay me for the lessons, but this,' he pointed at his crotch, 'you can have for free — if I feel like it.'

We met later at a *milonga* called La Nacionál. The building was an Italian social club from the early 20th century. It had the chandeliers, fans, and nostalgic mustiness of those immigrant times of hope and new beginnings. Many of the big *milonga*s were hosted by former community clubs — Greek, Armenian — where new migrants with brilliantine in their hair had huddled to watch amateur theatre in Greek, Italian and

Armenian, and remember their lost homeland.

'People dance the way they are,' Carlos said. 'You can read a person through their dancing. Look at her for example. Do you think she's happy in love? Do you think she deserves to be?'

A woman with a heavily made-up, porcelain doll's face dressed in black lace and black shoes with white heels revolved in the arms of an elderly man who looked as if all his Christmases had come at once. That was because he couldn't see her pouting face which wore a distant, harsh look of disappointment. The look said: this man isn't good enough for me; no man is good enough for me.

'Or them. Do you think they're happy together?'

A handsome, joyless woman in an expensively lacy dress danced with a man in a stiff brown suit who was trying very hard, but would never look like anything other than a fat rich kid at the cool kids' party.

'I know her. She married him not so long ago. When I asked her, what on earth do you see in him, do you know what she said? 'You have to live with someone in the end. And it may as well be someone with money.' Now she lives the Argentine woman's dream — a professionally kept woman. Of course he doesn't like her to dance with others. We don't dance anymore. That's the price, it comes as a package.'

'But what about love?'

Carlos spat out a cynical laugh.

'Come on! Love comes and goes but money is forever. This is the Argentine woman's motto. What more can I say?'

A large predator arrived at the *milonga*: long-haired and moist-eyed, he glided at the edges of the dancefloor, hunting for small prey. It was Ricardo — or was it Fernando — I was quite sure it was him. I caught his eye and saw a glimmer of recognition before he moved on.

'I danced with him two years ago,' I said to Carlos, 'And he made a pass at me. He's like a shark tearing through the waters of the *milonga*, smelling blood. Why is he like that?'

'Because something's missing from his life. People live out fantasies in the milonga, they play roles that compensate for what's not there.'

I went up to greet him at his table.

'We danced three and a half years ago,' I said.

'Really? I can't remember. Did you look different? Where are you from?'

'Last time I was from New Zealand.'

He laughed, but still refused to remember me.

So that's why he didn't recognise me. His wife was sitting next to him but he didn't introduce me. I was clearly behind with the news — it was hard to keep up with the doings and undoings of tango couples. He didn't invite me to dance. Suddenly, I doubted my memory. Perhaps it hadn't been him at all — all I remembered was long hair, but there were others with long hair. The real Ricardo or Fernando might have shaved off his hair. The name hardly helped. The supposed Ricardo or Fernando haunted the *milongas*, with or without his wife. When she was there, he sat next to her and looked like a grounded child. When she wasn't, he glided around the dancefloor or sat on his own, like a child without an ice cream. His face said: I know I'm never going to find the woman or the dance I'm looking for, but I'll keep looking anyway.

Carlos had a tango classification: there was the 'tango condom', which was predictable and dull, the 'double condom' when it was doubly so, the 'terminator' — a sociopath on the dancefloor, and the 'tango random' — when it was surprisingly good.

At our table, we browsed through the magazine *BA Tango*. A woman dancer identified four types of *milonga* men. The 'stars' were glamorous dancers, often professionals, and out of reach for plain women and women beyond 25 — because the cultural currency of the country dictated that female youth gave the Argentine macho prestige, just as male wealth gave the Argentine woman status. Fernando (or was it Ricardo) was one of those. Perhaps that's why he didn't invite me now — at thirty-one, I was too old. The seekers came in two types: 'hard' and 'practical.' The hard seeker hovered at the edge of the dance-floor, forever seeking the perfect woman, if not the perfect dance, forever moving on to the next one. The practical seeker was charming, but had an agenda: he looked for a lonely heart who needed him, and could gift him with her money and her indulgences. Sooner or later, though, he would tire of her, ditch her, and sit with his drink, lamenting woman's cruel nature, before he moved on to the next practical relationship. The 'eternal youth' contingent consisted of aged men desperate to plug into the fountain of youth. They only danced with the youngest available woman, and if she was a beginner, all the better — they would teach her, they loved to teach. When their wives, probably retouched by plastic surgery, attended the dance on the weekends, these men assumed the autumnal demureness expected of their age. Finally, the 'elite' were men who had it all. Sensitive yet free of neurosis, they danced with all women, regardless of their age and looks. They were cultivated, pleasant, unsleazy, in other words, a semi-extinct species. This was Carlos.

'I know,' he said with a theatrical sigh, 'I often feel semi-extinct. It's hard to be so perfect in an imperfect world.'

At my last *milonga*, Carlos said in between dances:

'Don't be sad, you'll only miss this until next time you come. Fortunately, everything comes and goes, but tango is always there. Lovers, husbands, professions, all come and go. Empires, historical eras, revolutions — they all fail, but tango remains. The Roman Empire fell because there was no tango. They had no outlet, you see, no close embrace to save them from self-destruction. All they had was sex. Tango makes us better, you see, it brings out the best in us. Sex doesn't. But yes, the Big Bang, Evolution, these are all details, while in some dingy salon the eternal *milonguita* keeps playing, and couples keep revolving under the chandeliers.'

'What was the world like before tango, I wonder?'

'I suspect the world was merely a rehearsal, a rumour. It was preparing itself to exist. Watch your back — here comes a terminator.'

the golden hour book ii

ALAN
GILLIS

ANGLICAN

When you put the salted cracker between your teeth
to tear it to shreds,
I thought of the breaking of bread
and rose-black wine beneath

a high and dust-swept nave;
of how stars of crumbs
glistened on my collar, gritted my gums;
and when your cold grave

complexion made of my mood
what your teeth made of the salted cracker's grains,
and your eyes stained like the rose-pink
window of that church with its bloodied nude

Christ lit up by a sudden chink
of light, I walked out into the pre-ordained
rain in hope of making you think
twice before opening your trap again.

SIFTING THROUGH

The plates shifted and her bowls moved,
you hump her dresser into the middle
of the room and waft a white sheet
over it, feeling like a removal

man in the middle of a removal,
then run your fingers over the wallpaper
as if investigating defective
workmanship, or time, as the wallpaper

wafts memories that wreathe and writhe
down to the shellacked floorboard's dust;
and you're drawn to the wallpaper's rot,
its mingle of oatmeal and cat musk,

as if, if you pressed your finger against
one of those dark blooms of blotch
you might lose it, it might poke through,
then your hand, your wrist, your wristwatch,

your arms to the oxters until you whoop,
whomp and clunter through the bright room
in shorts, clanging straight into the dresser,
back now against the wall, so that its moons

of bowls and plates rattle, quiver and jowl—
when she bursts from nowhere, built like a rake
singing whack fol tha dah will ye dance to
yer parner round tha flure yer trotters shake

with the bright light in her eyes as she scoops
you up and spins and the crisp papered walls
swirl and birl, swell and dizzy-spell
until you pass through all the days or all

the days pass through you, and you come to,
with a shiver in the gloam and start to re-veil
the dresser with the sheet, casting a spell like snow
which smothers all that is dream, and all that is real.

KONA
MACPHEE

LEPROSY
FROM THE BOOK OF DISEASES

Even the merest millionth part of blood
attracts the polished sensor of a shark;
the rubbery planet of a whale detects
a finger-tip's most transitory arc—

yet sense can lie (the elephant became
to six blind men a pillar and a rope,
a branch, a waving fan, a wall, a pipe;
the anorexic sees a different shape)—

and sense can be deceived (the phantom limb;
the dentist's prick of novocaine that stings
a cheek to swollen blubber, muted, bland;
the stage magician's dextrous conjuring)—

and sense can even die—imagine this:
to watch as tunnel-vision burrows in;
to hear, like Ludwig, music's dying fall;
to touch and not to feel another skin.

FEN TRAIN

a flock of swans, unshepherded,
grazes the chocolate soil,
their poise recalling long-drained meres
from which this ground was thieved

small runnels hold their stringent course
in high-walled ersatz banks,
while all around them, chastened peats
subdue themselves yet lower

the fencelines sketch geometries:
a rhombus, ploughed, and here
a box of ponies hunched in rugs,
their withers to the wind

now we take flight against a race
of pylons held in yoke
by rhythmical catenaries
that sag, swoop upwards, sag

then canted roofs of warehouses,
half-empty business parks,
a crammed pragmatic town, its new-builds'
vacant symmetries

now fields again, as rain makes slants
against the pane, defies
the dogged level of the land,
the blurred horizon's rule

to which each poplar perpendicts
its verticality—
a leafless plumbline to some star
the transient whoopers know

whose beacon spark might bode a tide
that comes to sink these rails,
these roads, these fields, reclaim this world
for water, wind and sky

PHIL
HARRISON

THE BIRDS, LIKE

'No, no,' said Mr Cunningham in his evasive tone, 'it's just a little...
spiritual matter.'

James Joyce, *Dubliners*

I found fourteen wee newts in the wee pond down near Jamesies, said
John Mac, sizing me up.

You look like a newt, I says to myself, but not out loud.

Your wee bulging eyes locked in tight behind your fat round cheeks.

His head rolled round like one of them dogs in the back of the cars.

Fourteen, I says, and he says, Aye.

And I says, Did you count them, and he nodded.

Really shiny, slippery wee things, he says.

His fat fingers darting out at me.

I gave him an inch.

What did you do with them, I says.

Nothing, he says. I tried to pick one up but it wriggled out of my fingers
and dived under the surface. Wee bubbles and all. I just poked at the rest
with a stick.

I'd like to poke you with a stick, I says to myself.

What colour were they, I says.

Sort of browny blue, he says. They smelled a bit funny too.

Did you smell them, I says, and he says, Well, like, yeah, you could just
smell them just being near them.

Why does your brother always fight, I says.

His fat head rolled up and his eyes stuck out even more.

Does he think he is somebody, I says.

I don't know. His head rolled forward and his eyes dropped to my feet. I gave him an inch.

I felt as big as a tree. I felt like picking up a branch and beating the shit out of him. I saw my breath on the air. Look at me, I says.

He looked up. His hands darted about for somewhere to stay.

Why do you think he fights a lot, I says, nodding.

His eyes filled up and he looked down again.

Look at me, I says.

He shrugged. He was about to cry.

Does he think he is somebody, I says again. I picked up a stone and fired it at a tree. I could fucken do this to you, I says to myself.

Are you listening to me, I says.

He just looked. Fear pushed his fat wee eyes out more.

It's alright, I says, it's alright. I put my hand on his shoulder. He went to move away but I moved closer. I could smell his breath.

It's alright.

He was looking up at me. I'm only a couple of inches taller but it felt like a mile. I pulled him closer. He squirmed.

He's a dick, I says.

He shrugged. Tried to. I dug my fingers in tighter, and he winced. This is what it feels like, I says, to myself. This is what it feels like.

I swear to fuck, I says, I swear to fuck if he tries it one more time I'll kill him. He believed me, John Mac. I believed myself. I knew how it would feel, the dull thud of my fist on his cheek, the echo as his body crumples, the raspy breathing as I dig my foot into his stomach, dust rising, him spittin, coughin.

You hear me, I says, you hear me. I fucken will. You hear me. Tell him. Fucken tell him, right.

And then I saw them. The birds, like. It was quiet at first, hardly anything, but then they were coming closer. Sparrows was it? 'Maybe sparrows.'

I let go of him and he fell, he actually fell, on his knees like, as though I'd been holding him up, like strings, but I hardly even noticed. I was looking up already, watching, waiting for them to come. It was starlings. There was one, two, and then they came, hundreds of them, I swear hundreds, and they were moving like there were threads between them, like they were tied together. They dropped, sudden, a dive, then rose again, glidin, like they weren't even trying and it was beautiful, it was so beautiful and I just kept thinking, all I could think was god, I wish I was one of them. I'd give anything. I'd give anything. John Mac was still on the ground, but he was looking up too, his fat eyes rolling and his mouth half open and he was half smiling, like, he was amazed too. And I looked from him to the birds and back to him and I says you alright. And he was.

NICK
HOLDSTOCK

A GOLDEN BOWL

Beijing, and he cannot sleep. Because of the time difference. Because of the nineteen floors of concrete being shaped next door. During the day, during the night, the sounds of hammers, drills, machines. The noise is loudest in the morning, quietest after lunch.

From his twelfth-storey window, Daniel sees it all. The basic shell is mostly done, its walls smooth, tiled in white. Inside is blank, not started, maybe not even imagined. Either they'll be rooms, like his, or office cubicles. Clues are on the red banner that hangs from the roof. Fifteen yellow characters are painted on its fabric, the last an exclamation mark, the third the character for 'big'. He doesn't know the others, and although some of them look like things — a square, a hand, a tuft of hair — most of them do not.

Daniel stares through early light as the tarpaulin flaps. Below, in enclosed squares and boxes, spreads the mesh of streets. He was in them yesterday and the day before; mute and ignorant of meaning; wandering, without destination; lost until, by chance or map, he found the hotel.

He has Seen Things. Roasted scorpions. Pretty girls spitting. Old people walking backwards. Street kids selling plastic flowers. Sparse rooms full of smoke and mah-jong. Everywhere, on big and small streets, in the parks and by the road, in ones, and less often, twos, men in cheap suits squat. Their feet are flat upon the ground; they have an air of waiting.

These sights and the things they promise. This is why he's come. Not to teach English. Not to save the world, or just the Chinese. He has come to look.

It is what he said to everyone back home: that there could be a country, with over a billion people, that we have never been to, and know so little about, seems not just strange but wrong.

Maybe he will write a book. So people can know.

The corridors are quiet. The woman at reception sleeps on three chairs pushed together. Automatic doors slide open and he feels the heat. It is like an old thick blanket he cannot shake off.

The hotel is on a small street. Left leads to narrow lanes, right to the main road. Daniel stands, undecided, confused by the scene. Although it is 6 a.m., he feels there should be crowds.

He looks both ways. Sees no one. He looks at his watch again then something starts to glide. It moves like a bicycle, but has more wheels and a trough in front. The trough is piled with cabbages. The rider is a man in clean blue overalls. Daniel stares until the man begins to stare back. When Daniel raises his hand, the man inclines his head. He does not seem surprised to see a foreigner.

Because the man must get to market. His short legs are tired.

Daniel waits until he passes, then heads in the same direction, past the tall white building that is finished only on the outside.

At the main road the farmer turns, then disappears, and Daniel feels this is somehow poignant because although, at some point between now and death, each may briefly recall the other, it is almost certain they won't meet again. He wishes this were a film, so the camera could rise and track, follow the farmer through the streets, to the market, through his long day, selling, cycling, until, with darkness, he was back home, in the village, in his bed, until the next day of the same when they would say *cut*.

Cars are passing on the main road, black ones and some red taxis with their fare lights on. It isn't quite the throng he wants, but at least there are people. Walking small, white, fluffy dogs. Carrying cloth-covered cages. Or shuffling in thick carpet slippers, hands behind part-bent backs, their old expressions slack. Beijing is waking up. It is like Act One.

The sky is grey and pressing, its clouds over-pregnant. A woman with two children nears, and he does not understand: he thought they could only have one.

Bicycles move slowly past, their frames long and heavy. The girls on them wear smart black trousers and were it not for his fatigue, he could probably keep pace with them by only briskly jogging.

Will he have a Chinese girlfriend? Everybody said he would; Michael said he *must*.

Then it's time for curtain-up. The shop shutters rise, on a cake shop, on a florist, on a he-does-not-know-what. There are vices, lathes and spanners; a smell of grease for a whole block. How is it they stay in business when they sell the same things?

And of course the street looks back. People pay attention in a city way. A gentle grazing of his surface; by no means a stare.

And then there is Arabic. Flowing cursive letters on a green background. It looks like a restaurant. It is closed. Daniel walks on, stomach empty, eyes gorged, until he finds a room where pans of oil and water steam. There are plastic stools and tables; all the mouths are eating. There are noodles, cakes, what looks like slime, and he knows this is the first of many tests. He has no idea what any of it is. He will probably make a mistake. Do something very stupid.

Maybe he isn't hungry. Maybe he can wait.

But if he leaves now, it's shit. He can't eat McDonald's.

Daniel practices the words. Then he goes over to a woman who has flat brown things. He points then says their word for 'two'. After a long, baffled second, the woman raises two fingers and Daniel nods, relieved. The woman puts two of the brown things into a plastic bag. Then she says, '*Wu mao*.' He hands her a five, she gives him the bag: it is all so easy.

Then she is standing, shouting, and he is afraid. She asked for five, he gave it to her. What has he done wrong?

He starts to back away, too slowly, she is moving fast. She raises her hand — as if to strike — and Daniel starts to panic. This is how it will be. Two years of mistakes.

Then he sees the notes. She laughs and does not hit him. He takes his change, says 'thank you' in English. He sits down to eat, and although it's a greasy rusk, whose main ingredient is oil, he eats it with pleasure. Because he has passed this test. He has got breakfast.

The only free space in the hall is above their heads. The seats, the space beneath them, every piece of floor and wall is claimed by people, things. He has watched it fill. Short, lean men with precious rope-bound boxes: their cuffs were frayed; their shoes were holed; their boxes contained DVD or karaoke players. Families, generations in a blur of overlapping features. Pairs of people struggling with bags so large that they each take a handle. The bags are made from chequered sacking that does not seem strong. Finally, in the last ten minutes, ones and twos of well-dressed people, couples or single men who all have the same suit (single-breasted, grey or black), the same hair (boyishly short bristles), the same need to snort and bellow into their mobiles.

This last group is the only one that really looks at him. The others are too busy with children, bags and sacks.

The floor is strewn with seed husks, paper, plastic, fruit skin, very small black bones. Meanwhile, people keep arriving into space that simply isn't there. There must be at least a thousand. Some of them, he thinks, must not be travelling.

Bells ring, then stop. Two blue uniforms appear and everyone approaches the platform gates as the train shudders in. Daniel puts on his rucksack and in doing so hits a woman, who sways and almost falls. 'Sorry,' he says in Chinese; she does not respond. He picks up his two other bags — he has either brought too much, or nowhere near enough — then looks over the heads. The uniforms are talking in a casual fashion. Occasionally one of them glances at the thousand people waiting, but neither seems anything but bored. Then Daniel sees, as they all do, one of their hands move toward the gate. He, and they, take a great step forward. But the uniform is only leaning; the heavenly gate is closed.

For five minutes they stand and sweat and try to hold their bags. Children cry. His shoulders hurt. Then the space in front is free and people start to run. Daniel, trying to do the same, knocks into several people.

Each time he says 'sorry'; each time they run on. As if he were not there; less than fully real.

On the platform they are climbing through the windows of the train. One man tosses in his bag; another throws it out. The carriage is full, as is the next one. Daniel gets out his ticket but it makes no sense. There is a 6. There is a 14. Which is the carriage? Which is the seat?

A blue angel snatches his ticket. She looks at it, points left. He follows the numbers until 14. Then there is a whistle and the noise of slamming doors. Desperately, he heaves his bags up the steps. He stands panting, his back wet. The corridor in front is narrow, blocked by Chinese people. He has to push through.

His compartment is the third one along. Three Chinese men are playing cards on the bottom bunks. They are drinking green liquid out of tall jam jars. 'Hello,' Daniel says in Chinese; 'Hello!' they say in English. Two of them make room for him; the other, grunting, heaves his cases onto the rack. It will be twenty-seven hours till they reach Changsha. He will be in here, with them, for over a day.

He thanks the now-perspiring man who stowed his bags. He looks at the four beds, the lowers, the uppers. Which of these is his?

The man pats an upper one. 'OK!' he says, with his thumb raised, as if, by the exclamation, he has made sure that everything — the journey, his new foreign friend — will soon attain this state. He asks Daniel where he's from, and this is one he knows. '*Ying-guo*,' says Daniel. The men nod sagely. The train shunts into motion.

He does not know if they expect him to sit. He does not want to be rude. But if he does, what will he say? They probably don't know English; it will be awkward.

But even though he's on a train now creeping through Beijing — past people huddled by the track, past lit boxes, silhouettes — he can still, as at parties, command his Powers of Escape.

The toilet, when he finds it, is a round hole cut from metal. Like the kind he used in France when his family went camping. It, like this, was a place to hide when the games got too rough. One afternoon he squirted two French boys with his water pistol. The first few times they didn't mind, but after four soakings they chased him to the toilets where he locked himself in. They banged on the door and shouted, but after twenty minutes, they said 'Fuck' and left. He waited. It stayed quiet. After ten minutes he opened the door. When he did not see the boys he felt a pulse of victory.

They were waiting for him by his caravan. They pushed him to the ground, then one sat on his chest. The other scooped up dirt and pushed it in his face. 'Eat,' the French boy said, and though he told his mouth, *stay shut*, it opened nonetheless.

The dirt was coarse and dry; he spat out what he could. When he got up, he saw his father. He was watching from the window with a glass of beer.

He is being silly. This is not the campsite. This is not his school.

Daniel opens the door and goes back to his compartment. There's no need to worry. None of them will bite. Or laugh. Put things in his mouth.

But his heart beats faster. There is an expectant silence from behind the door. He slides it open. Then, despite the quiet's best efforts, a sound manages to burst through, an involuntary noise, like the kind that children make when they are trying not to laugh. Not a full outburst of mirth; more a happy splutter.

They are snoring. Daniel removes his shoes. He climbs up onto his bunk and undoes his trousers. He shuts his eyes and gradually, the train rocks him to sleep.

It is not the same world. His doesn't have this ochre space that ignores the horizon. It has no river as yellow, or wide.

This, he thinks, is how they live here; why they have this wheat and maize; why they built these mustard houses; carved the lattice round the gables; made the roof slates look like scales (*fish*, he thinks, *dragon*).

There are mounds of stones like tombs. Men working with spades and hoes. Geese. Dogs. A sty of pigs. A way of life that's been the same for centuries.

Ravines appear, some of them with cave-like openings in the yellow earth. He thinks of people living in them. Cooking rats on smoky fires. Their hair long and matted.

His stomach has had no food since last night's biscuit dinner. There must be a restaurant car. He has seen polystyrene boxes dripping reddish oil.

Daniel walks through carriages that are just rows of beds. The beds are green, look hard, and go up to the ceiling. The people on them smoke, play cards, knit, drink tea, read magazines and newspapers, peel apples with small, sharp knives, lie on their backs, sleep, talk on mobile phones, crack different kinds of seeds with their teeth and fingers. Some of them look up at him but he just walks on.

In the restaurant car a waitress, who is very tired and pretty, asks him what he wants. '*Xihongshi jidan*,' he says, and without pausing she says, '*Meiyou*.' He asks for the two other things he knows. They do not have either. She suggests some other dishes but he does not know them. She touches her head and sighs, then she walks away. Perhaps she has given up. Maybe he won't eat.

She returns with a bloated man whose whites are smeared with red. The cook lifts his hands and laughs, then reaches to a box. From it he takes a plastic tub with a photo of noodles. He puts it in front of Daniel, then pushes his palm forward. 'Five,' he says in English; Daniel gives him the right note. As he leaves, he hears their laughs: he is the punch line.

It doesn't matter. He can look at the world beyond, where dogs are barking at the train while people stand and look. If they were going slower, or stopped, the people could see him too. He could be the first foreigner that they ever see.

The men in the compartment watch him eat. They comment on his chopstick technique. Through the miracle of mime (two fingers pointing down, a thumb) he is led to understand that it is very good. One of them picks up his book and starts to leaf through it. The man turns pages, moves his lips, and kindly shakes his head. He gives it back to Daniel, who takes it, relieved.

They stop in a place where the buildings are coated with grime. The polluted sky is just the thing between the factory chimneys. 'Wuhan,' says the mime-artist. Daniel checks the map. They are more than half-way. They will probably reach Changsha in the early morning.

Daniel resumes sentry duty, determined that on his watch, no splendour will go unmarvelled, no wonder unseen. He turns on his Walkman, selects Random, Repeat, and after this, until the dusk, the compartment and the men in it are totally forgotten. Slowly, as the train moves south, he sees the colours shift. In the flooded squares of field the rice is a new green. Deeper than emerald, brighter than lime; it is the colour of fresh plant blood. Even though it's late July, it makes him think of spring. He has left almost everything — friends, family, language, culture — that constitutes his self. And at first this is frightening. To have all the props removed. For the habits to be useless. But as the sun moves to the water, as the green is slowly gilded, this fear moves aside. Quickly, in its place there grows a rushing sense of *could*. Freedom. Possibility. The chance to feel and act the way that he wants to.

He'll be confident and kind. He won't be afraid.

The platform is dark and empty: they said they would meet him. Has he got off at the wrong stop? The conductor — slim, sharp teeth — said the word 'Changsha.' But she said other things, and maybe these were not *this is* or *next stop*. Maybe she meant *the stop after this one*; *in one hour*; or simply, *this is not*.

The train jolts into gleeful motion. It doesn't need to stay and watch this foreign boy's panic. In Beijing there was a ticket office where they spoke English. In this place maybe no one does. Which means he could be here for days. And what if something happens?

In the shadows, something shifts. He cannot run with all these bags. He does not know the word for 'help.'

The voice splits his name. It says, 'Mr Tit?' Then, 'well?' It does not seem convinced that these words go together.

'Yes,' escapes from Daniel's throat, and then, like a reluctant spy, the figure steps forth. A girl. Short, and on the podgy side. Her smile is chalk-bright.

'Hello,' she says. 'My name is Haiying. My English name is Helen. It is very nice to meet you.'

'Nice to meet you too,' he says.

'I work in the Foreign Affairs Department. If you have problems, you must tell me.' She looks at his bags. 'Can I help you?' She takes the smaller one and begins to move. He follows her down a high-ceilinged tunnel that echoes their steps. The light at the end is pale and seems to promise sleep. Just a few more steps, it says. Then you can lay your head.

At the gate, despite the time, a man demands his ticket. He's not sure he still has it. Maybe it is headed south. It will reach Guangzhou by morning; Hong Kong after that.

He goes through his pockets with a weary calm. This, he thinks, will not prevent me. This is not a test.

It is in his back-pocket. He gives it to the uniform, who laughs, then speaks to Helen. She does not speak to or look at the man, as if he has, through speaking, somehow disappeared. She leads him to a black car against which two people lean. The man has a vulpine face. The woman wears a white silk blouse with a floral print. She smiles, steps forward, and extends her hand. 'Hello,' she says, followed by 'Welcome.' Which is where her English falters. 'Nice to meet you,' she manages, and then the well is dry.

'This is Miss Yang,' says Helen. 'She is vice-dean of the Foreign Affairs Department.' And although this means nothing to him, he can tell from her tone, that this, at least for her, is of more than a little importance. 'Who's he?' says Daniel, gesturing at the man, who is now busy spitting. 'Is he in the Foreign Affairs Department?' The spit drop leaves his mouth slowly, in no hurry to gather, fall, join moistly with the ground. He looks up at Daniel, grins, then speaks in a shrill whine.

Helen laughs. 'This is Mr Zhou. He is the driver.'

Miss Yang touches Helen's arm, then speaks. Helen turns to her, then back to him. 'She says you have had a long journey. You must be very hungry. What would you like to eat?'

Daniel demurs. 'It's okay, I'm just tired.'

Helen translates, for Miss Yang, then him. 'She says you must. She says you are very thin.'

He doesn't want to, but he will. Because he is grateful. They load his things in the car. Mr Zhou offers him a cigarette, and sighs when he says no. It is a sad, strange sound that doesn't fit his face.

They get in the car, Miss Yang in front, Helen in the back. They drive through dark, narrow streets and nobody speaks.

They stop outside a strip-lit cube with plastic chairs and tables. Garish posters — flowers, kittens — shout forth from its walls.

Miss Yang and Helen wipe their chairs; Mr Zhou just sits.

Helen says, 'Do you like noodles?' Daniel says he does and thinks of lying on the floor. Although the light is very bright, there's shade under the table.

Five minutes later he receives a steaming bowl of liquid. Beneath a bright red slick of oil, a mass of grey worms wait. He looks at it till Helen asks if he can use chopsticks. He says he can, then picks them up. 'Aren't you going to eat?' he says.

Helen laughs. 'I don't like to eat in restaurants. I cook for myself.'

'Why not?'

Her whisper is unnecessary. 'I don't think they are clean.'

They sit and watch him eat. The food burns his throat. It feels strange when he swallows; as if his larynx has been coated with corrosive varnish. He drinks two glasses of boiled water. The sensation, like the dirt, will not be washed away.

He downs sticks after half the bowl. Miss Yang says something that Mr Zhou nods at.

'She thinks you should eat more,' says Helen. 'It will take at least five hours to get to Shaoyang. She does not want you to be hungry.'

'Really, it's okay,' he says, more sharply than he means.

Helen translates. Miss Yang frowns and speaks a stream of short, fast words. Helen answers. Then Miss Yang. Mr Zhou. Helen. Miss Yang.

Helen. He is getting tired of being discussed.

Miss Yang, for all her outward calm, has begun to sound angry. When Helen turns back to him he prepares for an ultimatum, something along the lines of eat-or-we'll-leave-you. Instead she smiles sweetly and says, 'Did you go to Tiananmen?'

'No.'

'The Forbidden City?'

He shakes his head, proudly.

'What did you do?' she says.

'I just walked around and looked at things. I'm not really interested in famous, tourist places. I prefer to see ordinary things, how most people live.'

Helen translates for Yang and Zhou, then says, 'You must be very tired.'

Miss Yang pays, then they leave. Even though he's tired, exhausted, Daniel stares out the dirty windows. This is the largest city in Hunan. It must have sights to see; things worthy of wonder.

They drive through deserted streets where the shutters are down. They pass abstract shapes of concrete on a roundabout. The city, if it has marvels, is keeping them from him.

It is only as they are leaving, as they climb the hill, and turn, that Changsha relents. A band of lights, and then the river, grey and moving through the black except for a patch midway where, judging by the fairy lights, a small island squats. Beyond the water, buildings tower, rarely with a flash of neon, more often as a sense that the unseen space is filled. The streetlights are greenish white. And then there are fires, small ones, probably local affairs that are under control, but in their distant shift and flicker, he finds a reminder. It looks like any other city, but out there, in the night, on beds, on floors, in alleyways, are Chinese in their millions.

They drive on a motorway which is new and empty. Helen asks about his family (what job does his father do? Is his sister married?), and he answers while watching the small icon of Mao Zedong that hangs from the mirror. Perhaps, if his eyes track its sway, he will fade into sleep.

A blast. Music, loud and from a speaker right above his head. It sounds like a saw. He can see Stan Laurel playing. Stan has a look of pleased absorption. He is playing for the minor joy of it. He would gladly play all day, pausing only to eat nuts or hard-boiled eggs or drink from a bottle. He would, were it not for Ollie. Ollie with the bully's swagger. With the hitting hands.

'It is called *erfu*,' says Helen, and then he's asleep.

The sky sucks a tongue of flame. The concrete cones are like volcanoes, and although he sees the bricks, the word is slow in coming. It is not until they've passed that he conjures *kiln*.

Dawn, in China, in this car. Another beginning.

Her voice is quiet and close, and maybe sarcastic. 'Did you have a beautiful dream?'

'I didn't have any dreams. Did you?'

'I didn't sleep,' she says, which makes him wonder what she was doing. He sees a thick book by her leg but cannot guess its contents.

'What are you reading?'

'It is about politics. Karl Marx!' she says grandly, then giggles.

'Is it good?'

Her mouth pouts air. 'It is useless. I only read it for an exam. I must pass it if I want to be a postgraduate.'

And this is interesting but... They are entering a town where the shops do not have doors. Garage-like spaces packed with boxes, crates and sacks, whose contents spill onto the pavement, lap as far as the road. Orange, red, brown, black, yellow. Herbs, seeds, nuts and maybe horns; creatures curled up as they dried.

'It is medicine,' she says.

He rolls down the window and the dessicated smells push in, mass and jostle in his nose. Later he will compare it to the ash from thirty kinds of incense. He'll say that it was 'perfumed to the point of cloying,' and then, emboldened by this phrase, 'that it was like the dust in a small room where a grandmother has died. You're not sure it should be disturbed but never mind, too late.'

In the fields, beneath the trees, Daniel catches teasing hints of water buffalo. In one way they are like big cows; in another, hippos.

They flash through a town that only contains wood. Helen is almost asleep; Miss Yang quietly snores. The road starts to get lumpy, which makes Mr Zhou speed up. Helen and Miss Yang sleep on for twenty shaken minutes. They pass a bus station then drive over a tall suspension bridge. A rusted barge is dredging stones. The water is the colour of a day-old jade milkshake.

Helen wakes up, rubs her lips, then sees where he's looking. 'A dragon sleeps in there,' she says. He does not know if this is folklore or joking.

The left bank is a wall of white-tiled buildings, which, although finished and in use, still seem temporary. Their windows are blue and mirrored, in most cases, barred. Some are shops, some offices, some are just dirty. The exception is a narrow red building with three stages of roof. A thin kind of grass pokes between the tiles.

'What's that? A temple?' he says — in disbelief, because of course there is no religion in China.

Helen yawns. 'A teahouse.' She looks at the street in an appraising way. 'Shaoyang is a very old city.'

Daniel, through his scepticism, hears that they've arrived. He can already feel himself looking in a different manner, with more than just the curiosity of someone passing through. These are streets he'll get to know. He'll climb those steep stone stairs, venture down these alleys. He may even go upriver; in the proper sense, explore.

The road veers from the river and moves through a market. The fruit and vegetables are too familiar. The same goes for the geese and chickens. It is only when they stop at a pair of closed black gates that he sees what he wants.

An old woman is leaning over a plastic bowl of wriggling things. She stoops to grab an eel then hits it on a piece of wood. She impales it on a nail; then, with a swift downward jerk, the eel is torn in two. The board is stained a reddish-grey; the eel keeps wriggling.

He stands outside room 3-12 looking at his watch. He would definitely be nervous, if he were not still drunk. He was on his sixth cup of rice wine when the red-faced Dean of English said, 'Mr Daniel, tomorrow you will have class.'

Daniel desperately grinned.

'Tomorrow morning. Oral English class. 2 classes, from 8 to 10, yes.'

'Fuck you,' Daniel did not say.

The Dean's mouth stretched. 'You're welcome,' he said.

Bells ring throughout the building. He hears running feet. He pushes the door, says, 'Good Morning,' walks, speaks without seeing, eyes almost completely closed, the same as when a cup is falling, almost at the point of breaking but you cannot look.

The roar of their reply — a forty-six-voiced blast — is thus a greater shock. The students are in two rows with an aisle between. Most of them are girls, but because they look prepubescent (despite being in their late teens) this is not a problem. They are staring with a look of unalloyed delight. There has never been a room of strangers as pleased to see him.

'Hello, my name is Daniel,' he says, then writes it in large capitals on the board. Hysteria. He can hear them trying to say it. 'It's very nice to meet you all,' he says, then perches on the corner of the teacher's desk. Delirium. Rejoicing. This, he'll learn, Is Not Something That A Teacher Does.

He spends the next five minutes talking. He tells them where he's from, how old he is, about his family, what they do, and although some girls at the front nod, he can see, on many faces, sheer bewilderment. His voice is too fast and quiet, their English too poor. Perhaps it doesn't matter. Perhaps it is enough for them to look.

'Maybe there are some other things you'd like to ask me. Think of a question, then write it down.'

Silence. Whispers. They begin to write, pausing to look at him, as if the answers, or rather, questions, were inscribed on him. Their faces are friendly, soft, as far away from threatening as he is from London. But the scrutiny still makes him uncomfortable. He looks out the window, down to the well-watered grass they must all keep off.

'Alright,' he says. 'Who wants to go first?' Suddenly their shoes, the floor, are truly fascinating. He waits for ten long seconds, and is about to pick someone (that girl with the awful fringe?) when a boy stands and says,

'Do you like China?'

'Yes.' They applaud. The boy sits down.

'Very good. Someone else?'

'Do you like Shaoyang?'

'Yes, I do,' he says, and they clap, albeit less. The boy, encouraged, stands again.

'Are you married?'

'No.'

'Do you want to marry' — he looks around — 'a Chinese girl?'

They erupt. They shout. No one has ever asked a more exciting question. They laugh and speak in Chinese; he begins to blush.

'I don't know,' he says, and they, as one, fall quiet. 'It doesn't matter to me where the girl comes from. I think there are more important things.'

He is certain that they're virgins. Nothing more than kids.

More questions. Does he like Chinese food? Can he use chopsticks? Can he speak Chinese? Can they be friends? Yes, he says, and then the bell rings. The first lesson is over.

In the break he eats two oranges. The students stare as if he were on fire. He has broken another commandment, perhaps about eating, perhaps about fruit. It is not his fault. No one has explained the rules. He won't get in trouble.

After the break he gives the students English names. He wrote these on scraps of paper when he was drunk last night. Mostly all the girls he's liked, plus those of family, friends, and then some random ones. He assigns the names according to resemblance. Alison and Lucy are the prettiest. Then comes Amy, Sarah, Ruth. Rachael, Emma, Charlotte, Sue. Owen is quiet and in the corner; Michael has his shoes off and a vacant stare. Claire is in the front row, smiling; Kat is somewhere near the back with well-combed, shining hair. The students accept these names with giggles of delight, and at first ask what they mean, until he explains, to their dismay (and in some cases, disbelief) that most English names don't have a meaning.

Impossibly, and yet, this takes up the whole lesson. When the bell rings he says Bye, and their bellowed, collective echo is such a keenly joyous sound, so full of happiness, so brimming with satisfaction, that even if it were at half strength it would still be wildly, grossly out of all proportion to the events of the lesson. They are standing, smiling, waving, as if they were on TV and had all just won. He has done this by the simple act of proving he exists. Despite the spreading hangover, his flat's lack of saucepans, its surfeit of cockroaches, Daniel Adam Titwell (BSc Hons. (2:1)), is properly happy.

The students file past him, smiling. Soon there is only one girl left. He watches as she picks up litter, starts to sweep the floor.

'Why are you doing that?'

She looks up. A pretty one.

'I must, it is my duty.'

He does not know what she means. He shoulders his bag.

'Lucy, do you know if there's a nice restaurant near the bridge?'

He waits while she processes. 'Yes,' she says. 'It is for *jiaozi*.'

'What's that?'

She frowns. 'I don't know how to say. Wait a minute.' She checks her dictionary. 'Dumplings.'

'Are they good?'

'Yes, very delicious.'

They probably are. But what they are, and how to order them, are still the great unknowns. The easiest thing would be if she came with him. No. That would be strange. It wouldn't look right.

'Where is the restaurant?'

She shuts her eyes. They open. 'Go to the bridge. You will see it. It is on the left.'

'Thanks.'

'You're welcome!' she says.

Daniel walks outside and across the moat. He walks between the blocks of flats until he gets to his. He climbs the stairs and puts the key into the heavy metal door. As it opens a cockroach scuttles underneath the fridge. A second realises, too late.

He spends the next hour arranging the flat. He moves the table from the bedroom into the small lounge. He takes down the kitsch posters in the bathroom and kitchen. Slowly, with each item moved, the place feels more like his. He surveys his domain. He has never had this many rooms all to himself.

The horn of his gut blows *lunch*. He goes out, down the stairs, then down the steep hill that leads to the gate. Everything looks as it did. The vegetables, the geese, the chickens. The row of small shops without doors. The woman, the eels. It is as if the tableaux had been waiting for his eyes.

Some students, who might be his, say hello as they pass. He smiles at them and walks the bend of the road. The river is chalky green, the sky above slate grey. Men are welding up ahead. They are trying to coax some life into a lump of metal. The pavement is grease-stained, bright-showered with sparks. One of them sees Daniel and nudges his friend. '*Lao wai*,' he says then laughs too loud for it to be a greeting. Daniel looks at their black faces and continues on. He repeats the word. *Lao wai*. He will look it up.

Daniel sees men playing Go; a woman carrying a fish; a cat tied to a tree with a short length of wire. Then he passes two teenage boys and hears a 'hell-lo.' The voice is high-pitched, the delivery slow: its speaker is fluent in the dialect of scorn. He turns and they are laughing. 'Hell-lo,' they say, delighted by this foreigner piss-taking.

He does not understand why they think it is funny.

A man with a shaved head is lifting skewers from a pan. The sticks have batter-coated discs. The man dips a large paintbrush into a tin of red paste. Daniel waits and watches the man paint the discs. He hands the skewer to a little girl with pink string in her hair. Daniel thinks that it looks nice. He takes out some money.

A minibus rattles by; a window slides open. 'Hell-lo,' says a voice, a boy's, a girl's, it does not matter. What matters is the tone. The whiff of locker rooms.

Daniel puts away his money. He continues on.

He can see a sheet of plastic on the opposite pavement. There are things spread on it, shoes, books, plastic combs, what seems to be a horn. It looks very interesting; he does not want to stop.

He starts to walk more quickly. Soon he sees the bridge. He passes a music shop, a bookshop, a shop of platform shoes. The last building before the bridge is a tall, pink-tiled structure whose glass doors are flanked by large baskets of garish plastic flowers. The doors swing out as he approaches, and then there are men outside, smoking, wearing leather jackets, pressing on their phones. Daniel steps into the road, and almost makes it by. But a passing taxi honks, and one looks, they all look. One says, 'hello,' two say, 'hello,' and then there is the anger, risen. 'One-two-free!' a fat man shouts; Daniel wants to stab him.

He walks on, but wants to run. He can hear them call.

When he reaches the bridge he stops to look downstream. He closes his eyes, he opens them. Maybe they'll get used to him. Some of them, but not the whole town. It will be like school, except he cannot hide. He will have to deal with it. Which will not be easy.

But he is older; he is an adult. This is a new place.

AIKO
HARMAN

LUNCH

Do you love me more than peanut butter
loves jelly? you ask,
as you spread a sandwich.

This is a good question.
I think, well they couldn't
love each other as much as

flour loves water, or *salt loves sugar,*
because these things are inseparable,
no longer distinguishable
once brought together—

and then I am thinking
of more intrinsic pairs.
Inseparables. Atoms. Quarks.
Animals that mate for life.

I look back at you, now cutting
the crust from the bread.

DRAGON SCULPTING

You do not know what a dragon is.
You have seen shows on telly
with dragons in them, you say.

You, just a ball of coat and dream-stuff,
throw your gloves into the wet sand and build.

You do not notice the ocean.
You do not know her sound or her smell.
You have never felt her cradle or rock.
You do not know that there are other worlds
with other beaches which are bath-water warm
or have seashells for collecting.

Your dragon faces the sea. You grunt
dragon grunts to Bass Rock as you build,
as a dragon might have when dragons lived.

As the afternoon flags into evening
and a cool orange paints your face
in sunset, you turn onto your haunches,
and call out to me to come see your work.

Your eyes flicker, describing
the sharp stegosaurus scales you made on his back,
the alligator's mouth with a seaweed ribbon of flame
spouting out of it, and wings which span
most of the length of the beach, bejeweled
with shards of glazed plates and rocks.

I take your hand and walk you to the ocean.
You see it for the first time.
We wash your sandy hands in the water,
and you shriek as the waves touch your shoes.

A dragon guards this beach, you say,
as I put you in the car. And you stare
out the window on our drive home.

RUSSELL
JONES

THE ELECTRIC

Officially, she was possessed,
under the control of Daemons;
couldn't bear to hear
the Lord's name

one   more   time

Fine. Threw her a Qur'an,
Adi Granth, Tantra, Sutra,
knocked her sideways with
testament, the line-up for AC Milan.

the   kid's   sick

She's thick, won't listen, can't see
her fingers for her hand,
hasn't seen the light.
She says, *switch on the bulb*.

HOW TO KILL A BLACKBIRD

I think I saw a blackbird in your eyes.
Not a reflection but the real thing.
I traced its black wings,
razor-beak, two coals set straight
for me, and the flash
of its breast-black streak with a black line.

Shriek and you're a blackbird.
You will be love for tails
and skies, so I'll be dull.
I will walk incognito
until that coarse caw courses
and I am given away.

Let me clip those wings from you
and splash your feathers like road tar.
Let me tear your narrow legs away
with my fingers; meet your skull
with my human heel; feed on
your onyx vocal chords like canapés.

The remains of a blackbird
are not the remains of me.
I will take the corpse
and burn it for you
so it exists as carbon
and is blacker than before.

B. 1984

First	Love	Sick	Days
Word	Less	Pay	Out
Play	Time	Off	Cast
Hard	Up	Load	Rate
On	Side	Bar	Rack
Top	Man	Made	Up

ROBERT ALAN JAMIESON

THE COMMISSIONERS INVESTIGATE
BEING A MEMOIR OF A JOURNEY TO THE FABLED ISLE OF THULA, JULY 1883

These last few days I have been thinking and thinking of the Nordland sum-
mer, with its endless day. Sitting here thinking of that, and of a hut I lived
in, and of the woods behind the hut. And writing things down, by way of
passing the time: to amuse myself, no more.

Knut Hamsun, *Pan*

I have recently read the new translation of Mr. Hamsun's novel made by
Mr. Worster and it has brought to mind an adventure of my own early
days, some forty years ago.

The Second Truck Commission Report of 1873 is a substantial docu-
ment and demonstrates the thoroughness of the investigation — yet it
had little actual effect. Commentators suggest that this was due to the
fact that 'complaints of the men themselves were not loud or frequent';
that they were so cowed by the oppression of their masters that they were
afraid to speak at liberty.

So the need for further investigation beyond the matter of Truck arose,
and the Crofters Commission of the following decade developed. Repu-
table men were gathered under the presidence of Lord Napier, to whom
they would report, and in the summer of 1883 a deputation took to the
sea in a steam-yacht — the *Prometheus*, chartered from the Lighthouse
Commission for Northern Waters. Sheriff Elfinston was chair, Lords
Cameron and Frazer-McIntosh his primary investigators. Their intention
was to call at a number of more isolated places in addition to the main
ports, and there hear directly the grievances of the people regarding their

landlords. I — Jas. Hoseason — accompanied them, as secretary.

By July, they had completed their exertions in the south of Zetland, and the Commissioners' yacht sailed to Thula, to the ultimate west of the Westness. Looking at the records I furnished them with, they saw that the two hundred and seventy inhabitants there paid a yearly rental, amongst them, of £140 to the Norbie estate. Of thirty-eight families living there, all were headed by crofter-fishermen, catching cod and ling from six-oared boats, and besides that, supplying crew to two boats for herring fishing out of Vass, at Berwick's station.

As the yacht approached the island, the sheer magnitude of Thula's cliffs astounded the Commissioners, appearing to rise from nowhere out of the Western Ocean, and growing a distant three-stepped outline, into a vast mountainous steep, towering over the vessel — appearing as it were, as Cameron observed, as a 'gigantic green berg floating northwards, having broken away from the west of Europe.'

'All manner of sea fowl seem studded into the rock face, like jewel seams in a mine,' said the awestruck Sheriff Elfinston.

The harbour was barely more than a cleft in the rock face, with a tiny jetty across it, and so landing on Thula was never easy if the sea was against it. Ships had been known to turn back many a time, with frustrated passengers and cargo undelivered, after an eventless crossing. But the Commissioners were blessed in this respect. The *Prometheus* anchored and they came ashore to a great welcome; it seemed the whole population of the island, including babes in arms, had congregated at the harbour to greet them.

They proceeded to the Schoolhouse in a great mass, the Commissioners glad to be ashore, ever more amazed by the isolation of the rock, led by the men of the Thula parliament; the rest of the population followed on behind as legs and curiosity could carry them.

It was remarked by one of the welcoming group, a Mr. Gaer, that no person not born there could ever shake the sense of being at the absolute outer limit of the world that Thula engendered — and that no Thula person ever felt themselves to be anything other than at the absolute centre of civilization there, while life on the Zetland mainland was at least one step removed from the heart of their solar system, and London as distant as Herschel's Uranus.

'No matter how dreadful or marvellous a person's deeds elsewhere in the globe, those are as nothing next to their conduct under the Thula fells,' another added.

The Commissioners had intended to hold their meeting in the School, but the day was so inviting that it was resolved to hold it in the open air and a table was brought to act as bench. With the Commissioners seated, proceedings began.

The folk of Thula, in readiness, had assembled their parliament, or Da Ting as it was called there, and elected this Robert Gaer, Catechist and crofter, and Mr. Andrew Robertson, crofter, to represent their views, as 'the best speakers of English in Thula.'

Robertson read the minutes of a meeting held on the 11th June at the Congregational Manse, and presided over by Mr. George Morrison, missionary, which bore that the Thulafolk had raised a subscription to send delegates to see the Commission at Larvik, should they fail to call at Thula while on their tour.

This memorial was to be presented to the Commissioners as a faithful expression of their wishes, in such an event, by Mr. Gaer, who now said the memorial in question set forth that the island lay in the Atlantic, about 26 miles from the mainland of Zetland, and was owned by the laird of Norbie. The factor was Berwick of Roovik.

The people of Thula respectfully submitted that their rents were excessive, and out of all proportion either to the value of what the soil could produce, or to the value of rich farming land in other parts of Scotland. They were unable to state the exact sum paid by each tenant, as the public burdens were collected along with them and they got no receipts; but as nearly as they could calculate, the best portion of the isle was rented all over at 23 shillings per acre for arable land, including the right to hill pasturage.

'The soil is very poor and exhausted, and owing to the perilous position of the island a large part of the crop is often either blasted by sea, or shaken and destroyed by violent gales,' said Robertson. 'We have calculated that on an average our crops do not provide us with bread for more than four or five months a year. All the rest we must buy.'

'In recent years the rents have fallen in certain parts of Scotland, but here no man has ever heard of rent decreases; it has been rising, rising, rising, for generations,' Gaer said, and added that 'Whenever church or manse repairs are executed in Vass, there is an increase of rent all over the Norbie estates to cover the cost, and that remains till the next repairs are called for, where increase number two is made in addition to increase number one.'

Gaer went on: 'The manse of Vass was built about 1867. Most of us have paid 10s. a year since towards its cost, and there is no indication of the charge ceasing. The people get no advantage from the parish of Vass. The minister is supposed to come to preach once a year, but is afraid of the sea.'

Commissioner Cameron then observed that even if he did come, he no doubt omitted to bring the new manse with him, and laughter broke out among the folk.

Gaer went on: 'There is no work to be had in the island. We must depend on the sea for our often precarious enough means of existence, and respectfully submit that it is entirely unjust for us to be charged rents that our crofts cannot produce, but which must be fished out of the sea. Even were rents more equitable, we would still be placed at a disadvantage, our situation compelling us to sell in the cheapest and buy in the dearest market.'

Robertson, a more placatory individual, intervened, as if fearing Gaer had spoken too forcefully: 'For a long time the landlord has been of a good type, and the factor as sympathetic and forbearing as possible: but we cannot tell how soon changes might come, and we respectfully submit that tenancy should be secured by something more than the good disposition of a factor, who might soon be removed.'

Robertson's assessment had some support amongst the people, but there arose a strange dissenting hiss from another quarter. He continued: 'As tenants we have nothing but praise to give the current factor. He has ever been considerate and merciful; and as islanders we owe much to the merchants for whom we fish, Messrs. Berwick & Co., Roovik. Whether we are in debt or not they always supply the necessaries of life, and they have done so in cases where there was little probability they would ever be paid.'

Though they clearly represented different parties, Gaer and Robertson both regretted that so many of them were getting more and more indebted, and were hardly able to pay their way year by year.

Thus united they respectfully gave the following practical suggestions, the considered verdict of the Thula Ting. Some of these would be mainly for the benefit of Thula, and others would largely be for the public advantage in the world outside.

1) That a substantial reduction be made on existing rents; and

2) that the power of eviction be curtailed by leases and otherwise; and

3) that compensation be given for tenants' improvements; and

4) that the attention of the Government be called to the very unsatisfactory mail service; and

5) that the necessity of obtaining a more suitable vessel be emphasised; and

6) that the port of departure instead of Gaerdirhuis be Vass, as that is much nearer to Thula; and

7) that in the interests not only of the island, but of the national fisheries, so advantageously situated a fishing station as Thula should be turned to account by the construction of a proper harbour; and

8) that in the interest of the fishing, and for the safety of the mercantile marine, a lighthouse should be erected here.

In supplement of this, Mr. Gaer handed in the following list of crofters' grievances:

1) The whole trade of the island is a monopoly in the hands of Messrs. Berwick & Co. and the inhabitants do not therefore enjoy the benefits of competition, and, although most industrious, are kept in a state of hopeless poverty; and

2) The want of fixity of tenure perpetuates this system by deterring competition; and

3) The want of a proper mail service retards the development of the island's resources. A small packet of about 14 tonnes burden at present carries the mail from Roovik. She ought to call at Thula once a fortnight but it frequently happens that due to the lack of a proper harbour there is often no communication between Thula and the outside world for perhaps two months at a time, which is clearly to the disadvantage of both the island and the world; and

4) The continued charge for building a manse at Vass, of which parish Thula is a part, and the cost of which we believe should have been defrayed long ago from the revenue derivable from Church lands.

Mr. Gaer went on to say that he trusted the Commissioners would heed the words of the Thula Ting, for they had thought hard of the best solutions. He also trusted that the Commissioners would use their influence in protecting him from any annoyance which those in power might feel inclined to inflict in consequence of his having thus given a true description of the condition and wishes of the inhabitants of Thula from personal experience.

Sheriff Elfinston replied that if his conscience were clear he should have nothing to fear.

Having listened closely to Mr. Gaer, the Commissioners then began to question him. When asked about leases, the whole company laughed.

Gaer said, 'There was never such a thing as a lease. Folk are tenants at will. There is none individual proprietor of his place.'

A voice from the crowd shouted, 'It is simply a republic,' and this drew laughter, to which Fraser-Mackintosh rejoindered, 'A republic without liberty?'

Sheriff Elfinston wanted to know of Gaer, 'Did not Messrs. Berwick offer to give up their business about ten or twelve years ago —and did the people of Thula not to a man sign a paper that the monopoly should not be given up?'

Gaer answered, 'Yes, I believe they signed Mr. Berwick's paper to fish for him.'

'Why did they do that if they wanted the monopoly to be broken up?'

'Because folk have been so long in slavery, not only here but all over Zetland, and are afraid of the evil that might result if they opposed the factors.'

At this bold statement, expressed with a burst of visible anger, a gasp passed through the crowd, and a dog began to bark, which was rapidly silenced by a guttural roar and the rise of another high-pitched hiss.

From the rear came a voice: 'If it hadna been for Mr. Berwick some of us would not be alive the day. He has done like a gentleman for us an we ought tae be thanksful tae him for it.'

At which several others broke out in support, met by more hissing. For a moment I was unsure what it meant.

Another man stepped forward. The Commissioners asked him to identify himself for the record. He said that he was George Morrison, missionary, not an ordained minister, but connected to the Congregational Union. He had been in Thula for two years and had attended the meetings of Da Ting in order to help translate their wishes into language that the Commissioners would comprehend.

'I have heard all the discussions and it is clear to me now that Mr. Gaer has gone far beyond his instruction in handing this supplement to your Lordships. His is not the opinion of the majority of people by any means.'

More of the curious hissing followed, and at this Sheriff Elfinston's at last called order, his patience done. He instructed Morrison to continue.

Personally Morrison thought that another shop on the island would not improve things at all, for there was so little profit in the trade with the island. Both businesses might give up were it to be halved.

Mr. Frazer-McIntosh asked if he considered that it was for the benefit of Messrs. Berwick that they maintained a shop there, to which no reply came. Then he added, 'Is it not a fact that the proprietor forbids any contact with other traders?

Morrison conceded that he could not answer.

Sheriff Elfinston wished to know about the religious habits of the people. 'Are many Congregational?'

Morrison replied 'Most of them. Indeed, few have connection with the Church of Scotland here, unlike the mainland part of the parish.'

'Which accounts for the strong objection to the rent increase for the Vass manse,' Fraser-Mackintosh nodded, smiling.

The sun was blessing the meeting and tempers improved.

Sheriff Elfinston inquired as to the level of attendance, to which Morrison answered that, 'They all attend regularly, though they are not as strict Sabbatarians as in the West Highlands and the Hebrides.' He was himself, a Lewisman, in origin.

'Do they consider it a sin to wander about admiring the beauties of nature on a Sunday?' asked Cameron.

'No, they do not. They are not so straight-laced as that.'

'Are they against such vain things as the singing of songs?' Frazer-McIntosh smiled.

'No, the inhabitants are very musical, very fond of sacred music. And their fiddle, of course.'

The mention of the fiddle brought whistles and cheers from the crowd. And so towards the close of the meeting, the proceedings took a conversational shape, with many voices speaking as they felt the spirit move them.

The Commissioners inquired as to stock, and were told that they averaged three cows and six sheep. None of them kept ponies, as only the proprietor was allowed that, which all complained of as the ponies would be very useful for transporting fuel from the hill where the turf was cut. At present the women had to carry it about a mile on their backs, knitting all the while as they walked.

They also said that they still had the fire in the middle of the roof, though none of them now kept cows in the family home as their forebears had done.

The soil, the Commissioners learned, was 'mostly peat and clay.'

Elfinston asked what crop grows best, at which a wag at the back shouted 'None of them.'

When asked about emigration, they answered that a good many of the young men had gone for sailors, and about twenty years ago a number of families went to a colony at a group of isles to the south of New Zealand, aboard a ship chartered by Berwick on behalf of the laird, an expedition led by the son of the schoolmaster at Norbie.

'Nane o those wha left hae ever come back hame tae Thula,' said one matron, perhaps thinking of a child of her own.

The young women, when asked, said they would never leave Thula. One explained, shyly, that the world away from there 'could never be home' to them and they could not raise their children in an unhomely place, for they would not then be Thulafolk.

'And how could a mother not belong to the same place as her child?' observed the most forward of them.

The young men, when asked if they would leave, said that if they had a powerful steamboat here, like the one the Commissioners had come in, to carry away the fish they caught to market fresh, they would 'make a lot more money and grow rich, and live well here,' at which the older girls all giggled happily.

The matrons and the older men then complained of the high price of certain luxuries. Sugar was 6d. per pound, while tobacco the men considered very dear at 6s. per pound. In response, the price paid to them by Berwicks' for their eggs was a pittance.

As to the matter of their diet, fish was largely used. In winter they had for breakfast, bread and milk when they could get it, but there was a great scarcity of the same, for want of cattle; sometimes just a little black bread and black tea was all they managed. They had fish and potatoes for dinner; but the potatoes were very wet, you could wring the water from them.

They rarely killed a cow, but ate their old sheep. They had no doctor on the island, the nearest was in Vass. But most of them had good health.

'Perhaps none the worse for not having a doctor?' observed Commissioner Cameron.

'Ah well, that may be so,' came the general answer.

'Potatoes and fish seem to make you as big and strong as we have seen anywhere,' said Sheriff Elfinston, and they all laughed.

'Or indeed as pretty,' Cameron added, 'as any of the lasses,' at which many of the Thula girls gave evidence of a little shiver of pleasure on their lips, and stared hard at the particular young man she had her eye on. Whistles followed, and much laughter.

This was a perfect note, Elfinston suggested, on which to conclude the meeting, and as the Commissioners at last fell silent, their questions done, the people all felt indulged by their closing kindness.

But then, just as they were preparing to leave the table, there stepped forward a very old man, a tiny wizened figure with a staff, who immediately appeared to command the respect of the assembly as some kind of tribal elder. He said in a heavy Norse accent that he spoke English poorly, being the last Norn speaker on the island, but begged leave to have his say. Morrison agreed to translate if required.

Lord High Commissioner asked who he was, and he replied that his Lordships might address him as 'Daldmana Thula,' which he spelled out. The folk all laughed, but it took me a minute to see the joke.

Though pressed again for his name, for the record, he ignored that. Instead, he continued in his heavily accented English, speaking very slowly, as if translating every phrase carefully in his mind beforehand, and I, who was minuting the proceedings, was able to comprehend him nonetheless.

'Most of us reckon James Berwick... a merciful man... though we are less sure about his older brother. Whatever name you may give... to the system... whether monopoly as you have termed it or godsend... he is our current means of... winning our living... and none of us would harm that. But the Thulafolk have forgotten the courage of their fathers... and no longer do they take wildfowl from the cliffs. In my bairndom... it was the fowling... kept us living... when other foods were scarce... and none of the young men know the cliffs... they have lost the taste for all seabirds except the pirisolan that they take with nets.'

The Commissioners asked of him what 'pirisolan' was and they were told it was the greatest of delicacies, being young solan geese specially prepared, and that they would have the chance to sample some after the meeting.

'It is a terrible waste,' the old man of Thula went on, 'Of the island's resources... letting so many fowl escape.' He spat on the ground and cast his gaze across the men assembled and they averted their eyes, as if they knew that he was right.

'If I was three score years younger... I would show them all... how to scale the Kame.'

The other men brightened at this, and muttered if only he could show them, they would gladly go with him. Gaer informed the Commissioners that it was the pox that wiped out the knowledge, there being only six fit men left alive when it was done with them, and none of them old enough to be cliffmasters. Routes had been forgotten and fear set in.

But the old man of Thula ignored him. 'I do not think that... these times are any worse... than the past. Life has always been hard and... it is true that the people... have been enlightened... as to the ways of the world. But... they require a great deal more light... before they make anything of it.' He drew breath, but none spoke, and he went on, 'Things being as they are, we must do what we can... the crofter has had a hard and bitter time... we work a good deal harder than many a rich man's horse... and we have had to do it keep alive our families. The crofters are the true strength of the nation... they ought to get a little more fair play... in time to come... than they have had at the hands of the landlords... in the past... but I do not blame them as much as the landlaws... that allow them... to behave as they do.'

The company agreed, bending their heads to nodding, as he spat again. 'Every man is selfish,' he said, 'And why not the landowners too... just the same as others. Yet something should be done for the crofters... and not only of Thula... I do not wish it for myself, but for the rising generation... it is not right... that a part of the British Dominions... should slave as if they were in slavery.'

At this he fell silent and the Commissioners could do nothing but nod in agreement. They thanked him for his wisdom and he departed as mysteriously as he had appeared, into the mass.

Then proceedings were terminated by the chairman thanking all the islanders for coming out to speak with them. Robertson, on behalf of Thula, thanked the Commissioners for coming, and hoped that they would not forget their visit. The Commissioners promised to give their memorial their best attentions.

The majority of the company arose and retreated a little, but a large number remained at a discreet distance, watching as the women then brought a selection of platters and the Commissioners were honoured by a repast of Thula delicacies, which they found interesting if sometimes indigestible — the delicacy that was the pirisolan lay rather uncomfortably in the stomach afterwards. The assembly began to drift away, once we had finished eating.

We then proceeded to the top of the high cliffs, and enjoyed a splendid lookout on all sides. We were shown a number of curiosities, and heard about 'Hell's Lum', a hole which descends from the heights into the earth and is reckoned to be 'bottomless, for none that had gone down there had ever come back, and must be climbing down still,' as one wag said. But the exact whereabouts of this amazing feature had been forgotten, it was said, like much of the old lore, with the plague and the death of the old Norse language. Though curiously they retained the fiddle of their Norse ancestors.

On descending again to the shore, they were followed by the whole population, who said their farewells in such fond measure that it seemed to the Commisioners they were parting from old friends.

The steamship sailed round to the face of the great cliffs and they all marvelled again at the scale of them, saying that they had never seen such steeps anywhere. The mass of seabirds gave off such a stench of guano that our stomachs were rather tested.

A great number of the Thulafolk had climbed the fell at the easiest point and were waving. Over the surface of the swelling water, from very far away, there seemed to come the faintest echo of — we presumed — some song of parting, though 'Auld Lang Syne' it was not. A few, probably the youngest and fittest, had even climbed as far as the shoulder of the great Kame itself.

As the sun began to move through the western sky the captain turned the bow of the ship away from it, and steamed towards Skalvaa. The commissioners conferred and agreed that, strange and ignorant of the world outside though they be, and naively mistaken as to the value and standing of their place within it, yet the Thulafolk had made a great deal of sense. There was, in their extremity and their methods of arranging their mental world to disguise it, something of the condition of all people.

'For is not everyone of us naive in assumption of our own importance?' said Lord Frazer-McIntosh, quite moved. 'Yet without that, how could one motivate oneself to live to the fullest of one's God-given potential?'

This had been the most memorable of the numerous hearings thus far, they agreed — and the pirisolan, particularly, was unforgettable. Some deep awareness of the condition of man seemed to be stirred by this outpost, and all were affected.

As the distinctive three-stepped outline of the mysterious isle slipped into the distance, the sun from the west shadowing it into darkest relief, now far to the north yet refusing to set, I was struck afresh by its remoteness, and was glad to see the lights ahead signalling the comparative civilization of the ramshackle little capital skirting the old Stewart castle.

This dominating fortress of Skalvaa sparked a thought in Sheriff Elfinston. 'Thula too is a variety of stronghold,' he said to Cameron, idly, as the *Prometheus* dropped the hook and we prepared to descend into the small boat which would take us safely ashore.

'But I rather feel the Thulafolk have opened its gates, and through us, wish to share their treasures with the world,' Frazer-McIntosh surmised.

'And is the world able to evaluate them?' came Cameron's response.

'We shall see,' said Sheriff Elfinston. 'We shall see what becomes of Gaer and Berwick.'

I picked up the Sheriff's baggage, and prepared to go ashore. The northern summer light was strong as we boarded the gig and drove through the rudimentary main street, where the commissioners then repaired to the hostel for gin and water, to restore appetites prior to supper. I found my attic room and transcribed notes while fresh in mind, writing late into the stillness of that long bright night.

I will not digress further into anecdote. Others too gave their testimony at the Skalvaa hearing which followed the next day. The complaints and the defences were as you have already seen them from the Thulafolk and Berwick's defenders. More than a few 'Robert Gaers' stepped forward, who told their own truth, and chanced fortune by doing so.

The meeting ran its course and the following day the Commissioners' steam-yacht sailed for the Orcades. But that is not the end of the story — for there appeared in the press later that year the following:

It seems Gaer was justified in his fear of 'annoyance which those in power might feel inclined to inflict in consequence of my having thus given a true description of the condition and wishes of the inhabitants of Thula from personal experience.'

Berwick obtained a decree of eviction at the Zetland Sheriff Court against Gaer a few weeks later — and, for good measure, added another for the sum of £40 he claimed Gaer owed them, demanding immediate settlement. The decree having been charged upon, Gaer had so little about him, besides farm stock and his few sticks of furniture, an officer was despatched from Larvik to conduct a poinding and rouping of his effects.

There is no lengthy account of the scene, unfortunately, for it would have been a spectacle indeed to see the officer come ashore at the island and march with his constables to the door of the Catechist, with the gathering crowd of Thulafolk around their heels.

Did the brave catechist stride out to meet them, or did he bar the door?

Were the children hiding, terrified, in the boxbeds, as the stranger took the furniture from the house and laid it out for inspection, prior to the sale? This we can but conjecture, but the outcome is on record: the officer was 'deforced; nearly the whole of the people taking part with Gaer; and although no violence was offered to the officer, the people refused to bid for a single item offered at the auction.'

The officer and his constables left the island disappointed, but threatening 'further steps.'

I do not know if there has been further outcome, yet the fortress, it seems to me, remains unconquered, beyond my ken and — by means of pacific resistance — beyond Berwick's law; whatever the fate of the players here. The very fact of living there, an act of ultimate defiance. I wish them well, those Thulafolk who live daily in the sublime, and would willingly see their advantage.

JANE
FLETT

FLAMINGOS

Cassandra was standing in the shower, perched on one leg, wondering about being a flamingo. The water was hotter than it needed to be, and painted a red triangle down her breasts and stomach like a give-way traffic sign. It trickled through her pubic hair and fell onto her foot. The other foot hovered in the air, keeping sentry. If she needed to leap out in a hurry, she could.

Actually, it was unlikely that thoughts of flamingos could help Cassandra now. It was too late to stand awkward and dumb, with too many limbs and too little grace. Perhaps two months ago, if she had statued herself at the side of the dance floor, monosyllabic and one-legged. Perhaps if she had balanced precariously near the end of the bar and raised one foot for running, prepared for flight. Perhaps if she hadn't let all that hair tumble down in a frenzy of gin and watermelon, and danced danced danced like wildfire. Cassandra's dancing limbs were always making promises to the boys who watched them. She had never quite caught on to what they were saying. Her extremities liked to get locked in private agreements in a language she'd never learned to speak. It horrified her to hear the suggestions when the boys vocalised them, but by then it had already been said.

All she wanted to do was dance. It had been a long day of pouring coffee and she was exhausted with talk, with smiles and exchanges, frothing milk, and what kind of career was that anyway? She was ready to let the music scoop her up and puddle her messily across the floor, spin faster and faster until everything was just streaks and traces, a blur of people and noise and the purple scent of cigarettes. She wasn't going to think of Nick. She would dance until her head was quiet.

Cassandra was reaching the level of whisky relaxation only accessible after work, where all the tension pings out of the body like a car engine, having covered 800km west, ticking and contracting in the driveway. The moment your entire body becomes an exhale, a cat's stretch. She was not thinking about the last time she slept with Nick, how he traced his paintbrushes over her hipbones, colouring her in.

'They're not pink naturally, you know, it's from the shrimp they eat. They add food colouring in the zoos to make them look more realistic.' A streak of fuchsia crawled its way up an inner thigh.

'So you could make them other colours?'

'For you? Anything. I'll fill the grounds with technicolour flamingos.' A splodge of turquoise round the bellybutton. 'We'll have one purple, fed on parma violets.' A smudge on the knee to match. 'Canary yellow, a diet of lemons and dandelions; green, that's easy, broccoli, lettuce, cabbage, all those greens; an orange one, orange with oranges, and carrots; crimson, we'll feed that one...'

'Carcasses?'

'Yes, carcasses. And then when you clap your hands, they'll swoop up into the air all a-flutter, and you know how they'll look?'

'How?'

'Brown.'

'Brown?'

'Well... yes. All those colours, mixed? Brown, of course. It'll be cool.' And his hand had smeared the paint together on her navel, and his navel followed, and then they were tumbling and giggling across the bed, smudging rainbows into the sheets.

No, she wasn't thinking of that now, nor about him drunk, giddy with his tongue in that girl's mouth. She closed her eyes, spun across the dancefloor, drilling her feet down, getting herself in deep. There was a hand making its way on her waist, proprietary. Twisting wasn't working.

Somehow, although she was turning round and round, the hand remained, its owner still before her. Looking to cash in his chips, her promises.

Cassandra hated to be rude. It was so difficult to talk to people you thought were pretty. Looking at a boy she liked could paralyse her, send her eyes to the ground to cower behind lashes and chew on lips. Even though they irritated her, she was quietly in awe of these boys who could try for what they wanted with such confidence. Surely it was all show and bluster, and one cruel word would break them entirely, ensure they never talked to girls again. People are remarkably fragile. She was terrified of being the one to break them. Most of all, she was terrified of causing a scene. But there were fingers in her hair and a tongue in her mouth, keeping it quiet, tucking the protests back inside.

'Hey... stop... I have a boyfriend,' she mumbled, looking for the magical password to extricate her.

'Shh. He's not here, is he?' He pulled her hair across her lips like a gag and kissed her through it, damp and fuzzy, gentle. For a moment, she almost liked him.

No. No, he wasn't. She didn't blame him for asking. What use were imaginary boyfriends who didn't even come out with you, who weren't there to stop you when your behaviour got out of hand?

Cassandra struck herself dumb. She stopped acting as a force in her own narrative, and let the night and the boy dictate what would happen. She discovered she had magical powers: when she closed her eyes, the boy disappeared. When she drank, she became invincible. When he pushed her thighs apart, she sighed and thought of red yellow blue streamers unraveling, and glass shattering, and fists, and fuck, jesus, FUCK.

She changed the third digit in her phone number and left. She got lost twice on the way home, ending up in neon cul de sacs and beneath the wrong bridges, cursing. Already she was beginning to ache vaguely, a metallic taste on her teeth. Her throat constricted with bile, too many cigarettes and a haphazard regret. Or a hole where regret should be.

The next week Nick apologised with a painting of her dancing, twirling like it was the last night of the universe, her hair aflame in strobes.

She couldn't tell him then, nor later that month when no blood came, nor now, when it was too late. She scheduled the appointment for an afternoon she should have been at the coffee shop, and the nurse held her hand and said she would be fine, honestly.

It didn't hurt. What came out of her was not flamingo pink, chubby and screaming, but crimson, and quiet. She stood in the shower until the water began to run cold, until she heard his key in the lock.

'Hell-llo!'

She put her dry foot down on the mat and stepped out of the water.

CLAIRE
ASKEW

It happened as I sloped home
across Meadows Park, shortcutting
through the rain. I was halfway over—
as far as I could get from street
or streetlight—high heels quicksanding
in the stew of soil.

FLASH

And the sky went white.
Not the white of eggshells
or snowfalls or saints—
not like the night's clouds,
or the waning moon
behind. The sky fizzed
like a flash-bulb, explosion white—
for a whole slow second.

Then dark again. I stood blind
and stunned in the sudden sucking dark,
remembering. I was five, on the Downs
with Dad and the dog and the dark.
Again, the sky—whitewashed,
split in the summer heat—
spilling over for a second.

And Dad with his keys
in his fist, afraid—
me, singing to settle
my stammering heart,
and the dog, lost
in the seething bracken.

DREAMING MY MOTHER: TYNEFIELD, PENRITH, 1974.

I dreamed that my mother and I
were 17, together
at Tynefield Comprehensive,
both cheated by the Eleven Plus.
My mother was pageboy hair
and slacks, poodle pins
and David Cassidy postcards, a picture
of Penrithian sophistication.
Her thumb-prints were black
from putting up papers
in her parents' shop—her feet
shredded from Saturday nights
squeezed into her sisters' shoes.

We sat in maths, side
by side—my mother savvy,
solving sheets of equations
as I sighed and struggled
with one. She whispered that
one day she'd be a bank clerk,
have babies and live by the sea.

Somewhere down the corridor
a cane cracked
across a thin white arm,
like the catch of a case
snapping shut.

And then somehow
I was in the road—my face
hot and wet on the white line.
My mother was spilled satchels
and screams, signing crazily
through shop windows,
waving down cars.
I was Karen, killed by a careless truck
at a turn in the road
as we traipsed home from school
through terraced streets
at seventeen. The reason
my mother sticks to the speed limit,
even today—Tynefield, 1974,
still trying to save me.

RYAN
VAN WINKLE

Cords of wood, lines of concrete, aluminum
slats covering new houses. Mortar
between pavement and cobblestone, endless
bricks raising, connections of lawn and mansion.
Her face

       was a new skyscraper; Chicago
at night. Sunglasses on the dancefloor.
Now she throws food on the ground for a cat.
The cat finds a dog and gums his tail.
She opens

       doors all over the house,
opens windows and the house breathes
like the soil connected to the crop.
She says, let the dust dance
in the shotgun

       beams. Her chair, her needle, wool,
she says, are only objects now. Her garden
inhales damp air at night, exhales
during the day. Watch the shore, she says,
the ocean

       is a lung. Watch the garden
from the atmosphere of the roof. She used
to sit in the club wearing sunglasses, watching
the cats connect with dogs. She used to rock
on her chair connecting wool to wool.
But then

       she had to open her house up
connect it to the dry air, the soil.
Had to bury her dog to help flowers grow.
Sometimes

       she watches his crucifix and tries
to see God where wood connects to wood.

OPEN THE CONNECTIONS, SHE SAYS

WAITING FOR THE OCEAN

Cover myself in blankets
of dust. Cover myself

in a second-hand poncho
Virginia Woolf could have worn

with her pockets turned inside out,
the light tongues of fabric licking

at the salted California sun.
It can take some time

and she keeps saying
she was drawn to me.

There is an attic of time which I hide in, time
where we walk blank beaches that never get cold,

visit bright houses which cast no shadows
onto pink shores. We pause on the coast,

her hands freckle and brown
and her hair lightens a little.

People say to her—*You
look good.* And I say—

*The chairs were flying.
They came for my head.*

And I say, *I was drawn to you
by the chairs* and she understands

and never calls the weather mundane
or melodramatic. And the ocean stays

in front and below:
unknown and living with us.

THE APARTMENT

Our new walls,
empty in the dusk,
hang like sheets
before first light.

There is a driven nail
by the stove that could
hold a pan if the walls
stay sturdy. And the

old tenants left a mirror in the
bedroom which looks back at
staring walls with fine cracks
like a museum's basement vase.

There are brown smears
in the study; chocolate, blood
or shit, we don't   know what
will happen to us here or what

will settle on rented walls
or if nothing will settle
at all. We've just moved

and already we are bitter
cranberries in each other's
mouths, biting about photos,
the place of the table, lay

of the bed. The apartment is a City
Hall we cannot fight. So we turn
like lawyers, against each other,
let the walls stare. There is a mirror

to look into, a nail to hang onto.
Our unopened boxes hide in corners
and closets like beaten children.
And we will take the blood

off the walls and the dust
from the shelves. We have one
year together in a place that
is empty at dusk, and feels like fog

       inside and between us
       so I cannot see you, and Christ,
       tomorrow, we will live here.

LINDSAY
BOWER

WHAT IT'S LIKE WHEN YOU'RE OLDER

It was a Saturday in October when Taryn wanted to go to Wadmalaw Island. We'd decided we were going to go after work, after we'd both cashed out and had a drink at the bar. The drink wasn't a necessary part to the whole equation, but it was what we did most days after work, and it was like our minds wouldn't rest if we didn't think we had that one thing waiting on us at the end of a shift.

'It changes everything,' Taryn said to me one day when I was cleaning out the giant metal vats of sweet tea. Undissolved sugar trickled down my wrists into the sink, and I looked at her like I didn't know what she was talking about.

I thought for a second she might have been talking about kids, because she was nineteen and had a son, but for the most part she acted like she was nineteen, not like she had a son.

'It?' I asked.

'I can't say right now,' she said.

'You can't do that,' I said. 'You can't say something like you're talking to me and then act like you meant to just say it to yourself.'

'If you give me a ride out to Wadmalaw sometime next week, you'll figure it out.'

She always acted like every friend she'd ever had had deserted her for some reason or another, and every now and then I thought I'd figured out why — because they probably had. I think about that day a year or so ago sometimes, when she asked me for a ride after work, and if I'd said no instead of yes because I felt sorry for her, I don't doubt she'd have latched on to somebody else.

It wasn't like I was special to her, because we could all tell she wanted to be liked by everybody at the restaurant, and I'd seen plenty like her that had come and gone before. She agreed with everything you said and laughed at all your jokes, and before people knew it, they'd been fooled into being friends because it was too late to ditch her without feeling guilty.

The kitchen guys made fun of her, but not a one said no when she got drunk at the bar and asked for sex, and when she told me she'd already done it with my crush Anthony, we sat out back with the blind dishwasher and cried. She cried because she didn't want to be a slut; I cried because even at my age, I still thought you had to be pretty to be a slut, and had only just realized that wasn't true.

'You wouldn't want to be one,' she'd said to me that day. 'It's hard work.'

'Don't be a slut then,' I said, 'and give me one of those cigarettes.'

I remember we both laughed, and when she asked if she could have the party of five coming in at six, I said yes, mostly because I didn't want to hear she needed the extra tips to buy diapers or baby food.

'I did all right today,' she said on Monday, once we were seated out back, counting our tips. 'I started doing this thing after last week, where anything I make over a hundred is mine for fun, and then I count my fun in sets of fifty.'

'Sets of fifty?'

'Fifty dollars. I made two hundred, it means I've got double the fun to play with.'

'Why fifty?'

'Take me to Wadmalaw on Saturday night. Come on, I had to take a taxi last time and it cost almost sixty dollars,' she said.

I didn't say anything, because I didn't want to drive her to Wadmalaw, and she kept talking like she didn't want an answer anyway.

'I told Bridges it cost sixty and he said I should have taken a gun. Then the guy'd be giving me sixty dollars to get the hell out of his cab. But I told him Lymon needed a mom on this side of the bars.'

She kept flipping through her stacks of dollar bills, then looked up.

'Come on. Take me out there. You don't have to stay I don't guess. But you'll want to when you get there.'

Whatever was in Wadmalaw must have been worth sixty dollars, so I told her I'd drive her next Saturday. My reasons were selfish because I wanted to know what the hell was in Wadmalaw, but so were hers because I know she could have cared less if it was me who drove her out there.

On Tuesday at five, just when we were about to finish up and the staff was about to change over, Taryn came around the corner into the kitchen with two shots of Jägermeister. I was putting the lid back onto a tub of fresh coleslaw I'd just refilled, and looking at the mayo and then up at the shots made me feel sick.

'I just got a call,' she said. 'We can go early on Saturday. Status said we could come over early and then I thought you and me could go to the beach or something.'

'Who's Status?'

'My friend. It's a nickname.'

'We both have to work lunch on Saturday.'

'I already asked Walt if we could switch with Chris and Big Rob and he said yes 'cause he's pissed they didn't show up for their last training session.'

She handed me the shot and smiled, her eyes shooting over to Anthony when he walked past, and then back to me.

'I saw that,' I said. 'I don't give rides to sluts. Gas ain't cheap, you know.'

'Sorry,' she said, and I could tell she really was even though I was just kidding, but then she was probably just scared I wouldn't give her a ride.

'Let's go sit at the bar. Maybe Darryl will let you drink in a real glass tonight,' I said, knowing full well he wouldn't give her anything but a plastic tumbler because she was underage. I don't know why her stumbling out of the bar four out of five nights was any less of a risk, but it was his job, not mine.

We walked over to the bar and sat down, Taryn wiggling to get up on the seat because she was barely five feet tall. Her skirt was so short I could see her white, dimply thighs hanging over the sides of the bar stool. I looked away and up at the television blaring baseball behind the bar.

'I read about a drink called a Manhattan,' she said. 'I think I'm going to try one tonight.'

'Darryl don't know how to make a Manhattan, and I wouldn't push your luck 'cause you're lucky to be getting a drink in the first place.'

'I want to branch out. I'm tired of screwdrivers.'

'You've already got a kid. Branch out when you're thirty,' I said.

When Darryl came around we both ordered vodka and Sprites, and I nodded so he'd know to put a little more vodka in mine.

'Let's take a shot,' she said.

'Okay. You're buying.'

She asked Darryl for two more shots of Jägermeister, and he looked at me first, like he was asking permission.

'I'm not her mother. Don't look at me like that,' I said. 'I'm thirty-seven, not forty-seven.'

We took the shots, and I lit myself a cigarette, then lit another one for Taryn off my own. She was near the end of her drink and I could tell she was already tipsy. Her arms hung down at her sides in between sips and she had the bedroom eyes of a drunk girl on the prowl.

'Will you be mad if I get with Anthony again?'

'If Anthony wants you, I don't want Anthony. So, no, there's nothing to be mad about,' I said.

'Was that mean? I can't tell with you sometimes,' she said.

'No, that wasn't mean. It was the truth.'

'Yeah, I guess,' she said, looking up at the baseball and taking a drag off her cigarette.

'Somebody's smoking Basics,' she said all of a sudden, looking around and sniffing the air. 'I'd know that smell anywhere. Rank and cheap. My daddy always used to smoke Basics.'

'I think Basics are the cheapest cigarettes you can buy,' I said.

'You know what's funny? That smell makes me think of my mama's perfume too, because I used to spray it on all my clothes when I was little so they wouldn't smell like my daddy's Basics.'

She laughed and looked back up at the baseball.

'He always had one cigarette in his mouth and another one resting in the ashtray.'

'Did he die of lung cancer?' I asked. 'Because I'll need to know what it's like to be tied down to an oxygen tank.'

'No, he shot himself,' she said. 'But it's okay. I was, like, five.'

She stubbed her half-smoked cigarette out, and lit another one because she could.

At one in the morning, things started to wind down, and Darryl did what he always did — turned off half the lights in the bar and played jazz — to lull the die-hard partiers into a drunken stupor.

I was tipsy and Taryn was drunk, but I had almost twenty years and twenty pounds on her, so it would've been scary if it'd been the other way around. She had coaxed Anthony out of the kitchen and into sitting next to her, and she had her arm lazily swung over his shoulder.

'You don't have to give me a ride tonight,' she said.

'I figured that out when we sat down.'

She didn't hear me, because she'd already leaned over to whisper something in Anthony's ear. He looked at me, but I looked up at the baseball, thinking it must be the longest game ever played.

I put a few bills down on the bar, and gathered up my apron and pens. As I slung my purse strap over my shoulder, my phone went skidding across the floor of the bar and a pen went flying under Taryn and Anthony's bar stools. I ran over to pick up my phone and I saw Taryn jump down to get the pen.

'Hey, come here. I've got your pen,' she called from across the room.

I walked back over and held out my hand.

'I like those pens. Us lifers are real particular about our pens,' I said.

She uncapped it, grabbed my hand and started drawing a heart in the middle of my palm.

'Let's get tattoos tomorrow after work,' she said. 'See you in the morning.'

She closed my palm around the pen and turned back to Anthony, letting her hand rest on his thigh.

When I came into work on Wednesday morning, Taryn was wiping down the tables, and had already refilled the salt and pepper shakers. She was wearing the same short skirt she'd had on the night before, and there was pep in her step, but her eyes were bloodshot and heavy.

'Did you go home last night? I guess not,' I said.

'I went to Anthony's. Lymon's at his dad's,' she said, scrubbing at some candle wax that had hardened on the one of the tables.

'I hate it when parents let their asshole kids play with the candles.'

'I'm going to cut fruit and make some coffee,' I said. 'Do you want some?'

'No, thanks. Hey, I wasn't kidding about the tattoos, you know. I'm ready if you are. We should get matching ones.'

'I've never gotten a tattoo,' I said. 'That's commitment and I don't like commitment.'

'You'll remember me forever,' she said. 'Come on.'

'If you think of something good by the time we're done, I'll do it. And when I say good, I mean I think it's good too. But I'll go with you to get one done if you want.'

'I already thought of something. You'll really want it. I promise. Here,' she said, reaching into the front of her apron and pulling out a piece of paper.

'It's just a star. You can't say no to that. It's small.'

I stopped wiping down the table as she handed me the paper.

'You know, like wishing on a star,' she said. 'You get a wish if you get one done. We can get them on our right wrist. That's a nice place, I think.'

'I'll think about it.'

'Come on. Say yes, or I'll be too nervous to do it.'

I thought about how stupid I thought tattoos were, because I'd never seen the point. There's nothing one-of-a-kind about anything these days and ideas always come from somebody else who had it first.

'Yeah, okay. We'll go after work,' I said. 'But tomorrow — there's sixty on the books and I know I'll be too tired later.'

'I have to be home tonight by seven to watch Lymon anyway.'

I turned to walk away.

'How were you planning on getting a tattoo today?' I asked, turning back and remembering her kid just then, because it was easy to forget something you never see and barely hear about.

'He's with the babysitter. She don't have nowhere to go. She's sixteen.'

On Thursday, before we'd left, Walt and the kitchen guys made fun of us when they found out we were getting matching tattoos, and Bridges called me a lesbian. I told them to fuck off, only Taryn was getting a tattoo, even though I told her I was getting one too.

'You seem happier,' I said, and I don't know why I said it, because I hadn't thought it until right then.

We were in the car and it was pouring rain outside.

'I am,' she said, rolling down her window a crack to smoke.

'Why? Because you got fucked? Don't get my seat wet with the window like that.'

'No. I just am. Everything seems different. Better,' she said.

'Well tell me your secret.'

'I would. But I don't really know. I feel older. And I think that feels better than being young.'

It took ten minutes to drive across the bridge to the only tattoo parlor in the city, because it was still damn difficult to open one, even though they were legal now. Once we pulled up, Taryn started looking at her wrist like she didn't want to go through with it.

'We're here. You can't back out now,' I said.

'Speak for yourself. I wasn't going to.'

We walked in, and when Taryn showed him the piece of paper with the star on it, the pierced guy behind the counter looked bored.

'Who's first?' he asked.

'Her,' I said.

'Come on, then.'

He started walking toward the back and I heard him ask Taryn where she wanted her tattoo.

'We want them on our right wrists. Here,' she said, and I saw her point to above her palm.

'I know my right from my left,' I heard him say.

Taryn came out not ten minutes later, waving a bandaged wrist in the air.

'Your turn,' she said.

I got up, and realized I wasn't thinking enough about this, but thought I'd look stupid backing out now.

Once we were in the back, he began setting up his work station, taking out equipment and squeezing ink into a small circle. The place was like a doctor's office, and there was a poster on the wall of a man with each of his piercings labeled.

'You ever had a tattoo before?' he asked.

'No.'

'This is the kind of tattoo people get when they've never had a tattoo before.'

'I don't even want this tattoo,' I said.

'Is she your girlfriend?' he asked.

'No, asshole. Just do it.'

'Why are you getting matching tats done then?'

'We're not. I want mine on my shoulder,' I said.

On Friday, Taryn had just about forgiven me for not getting the tattoo on my wrist. I told her nobody would call us lesbians anymore, because nobody would even know I had the tattoo, and she called me a bitch.

'I'm not sitting with you at the bar tonight,' she said.

'I wasn't going to ask you to.'

'But you're still taking me to Wadmalaw tomorrow.'

'What time?'

'Pick me up at eleven,' she said, turning to walk back into the kitchen. 'Oh, and I moved out last night. I got my own place, so remind me to give you directions.'

I left right after work, and thought about getting a bottle of wine and going home to drink the whole thing in peace and quiet. I'd go to sleep at eleven and get up at eleven the next morning, so I could be late and blame it on Taryn's bullshit directions.

On Saturday morning I was late when I finally pulled into the apartment complex. Taryn was sitting on the steps outside smoking a cigarette, impatient and bouncing her foot up and down.

'It's only noon,' I said, once I'd gotten out of the car.

'I told Status we'd be there by 12:30. We'll be an hour late,' she said, looking down and picking at the blue polish on her big toe. 'He might not be there and then we'll have to wait. And we were going to go to the beach.'

'I didn't bring my bathing suit,' I said.

'It's October. We're not going swimming,' she said, looking up. 'I just thought we could hang out and drink beer.'

'Which I'll have to buy.'

'Yeah, and I'll give you five bucks, so let's go.'

We'd driven for ten minutes, not talking, but with the music loud, when Taryn reached to turn down the radio.

'When we get there, just wait in the car,' she said. 'It'll only take a few minutes.'

'If you're having me drive you all the way to Wadmalaw to buy pot, I'm going to peel out of the driveway as soon as I see you walk out of that guy's house. There's a thousand people selling the same thing right here in town.'

'Here, pull in here,' she said, pointing toward an upcoming gas station. 'We can get beer here and I need some more cigs.'

'You don't need more cigs. You been chain smoking like a girl who doesn't really smoke,' I said.

I pulled into the lot and parked in front of the entrance.

'I feel neon,' she said, once I'd turned the car off.

'Who'd you hear say that? Because that's not something you'd say,' I said.

'Some show I was watching on TV. This girl said it. I like it, though.'

I got out of the car, slammed the door shut, and leaned down into the open window.

'People will always know you didn't come up with that.'

'Yeah, I know. So what,' she said, looking down at her pack of cigarettes, scrunching her eyes together to read the warning label.

'Maybe I should get lights,' I heard her say as I walked away.

It took us an hour to drive to Wadmalaw, and neither of us said much along the way. Taryn turned the radio down one more time to tell me to look for a house with a toilet out front — that there were plants growing out of an old toilet — and that's how she knew that was the right house.

Once we got near, I could see the house from down the road, and there were four or five cars parked outside. The house was brown, with a pine straw lawn, and looked just like all the other sad houses around it, except that it had a toilet out front and a mattress strung up on cables between two trees.

'It's better than a hammock,' said Taryn.

The mattress was stained and soaked through from rain, and I told her I'd rather go somewhere that had a hammock, because there's no way a place with a hammock would have a toilet out front as a potted plant.

'Just wait here. It'll take about two seconds,' she said.

She was in and out in just under thirty, and I hadn't expected her to be, so I was ready to act irritated.

'Let's go to the beach,' she said. 'We can come back later for the party.'

'I'll see how I feel after the beach and that case of beer.'

I pulled out of the driveway and drove back up the road.

'What did you get?' I asked.

'Pull over, right there. There's a beach access sign.'

There were no other cars parked, and I could see the beach was deserted; the sky was gray and looked like rain.

'It's kind of cold to be hanging out on the beach,' I said. 'And windy. It'll be hard lighting cigs.'

'Here,' she said. 'I want to show you something.'

She dug into the pocket of her denim shorts, and I looked away when I saw her thighs spilling out on either side.

'You should wear shorts that fit,' I said, not looking at her.

'I know. I keep hoping if I wear them while I'm trying to lose weight, it'll make me not eat all them french fries at work.'

She had something in her hand, her fingers closed around it.

'We should do most of it here,' she said, handing it to me. 'You know how people are at parties.'

I looked down, and I knew what it was before I looked.

'It's like a thank you for being my friend, you know? And I thought the other day we don't really know nothing about each other and this'll be our bond.'

'You don't have to go all the way out to Wadmalaw to buy coke,' I said, and felt dumb for being duped and stupid enough to drive all the way out to bumfuck for her to get a fix.

'Status is Cousin Kenny's best friend and Kenny said his shit's the best. And Kenny don't like me doing drugs unless it's with family.'

'I'm not family,' I said.

'You might as well be. We got the same tattoo.'

She laughed a little, and smiled at me.

'You know what I was thinking about the other day? The top five best things in my life. I made a list of the top five things that have made me happy,' she said.

We were sitting on the dunes, looking out to the ocean and there wasn't a single soul in sight. Our minds raced a mile a minute, and I was thinking about my life too.

'I feel like you get it,' I said. 'And you're a good girl. So don't fuck that up, because that's all you got.'

'I feel like I get it,' she said.

'You do.'

I lit two cigarettes at the same time, one for me and one for her.

'Now tell me about the top five best things in your life,' I said. 'And then I'll tell you mine.'

'The first one is this crush I had in seventh grade. I get older and older and do more and more guys and I don't think I'll ever feel that way about anybody again,' she said, and I thought about laughing, but she wasn't, so I didn't.

'The second thing is when I wrote this essay for my English class my senior year. I got an A and I really tried, so it was good.'

'Those'll both get replaced in ten years, I promise you,' I said. 'I can't even remember what it's like to write an essay.'

'You want to sit on the towel? Here,' she said, scooting over, so I wouldn't have to sit in the sand anymore.

'Now the third thing is dumb, I know,' she said, 'But when I went to a club for the first time, and man — all the boys and all the booze and all the lights — nothing's better than loud music and booze.'

'You stop wanting to go to clubs when you get to be my age. Everyone's younger than you are and it makes you feel old. So you sit at a bar instead.'

Taryn reached for another beer, and pushed a can toward me. I shook my head, and held up a full one.

'The fourth thing is my cactus,' she said. 'I've had it since I was five and it's still alive.'

'Maybe if you had a dog that long, but those things are supposed to be alive for twenty years — even if you don't water it,' I said.

'It's got pink flowers sometimes.'

'You know what I just thought, looking at you? You've got a face that you can tell what it'll look like when you're older,' I said. 'I mean, really, that just popped right into my head and I can see it plain as day.'

'Tell me what I'll look like when I'm forty.'

'Like you do right now, only happier. Because I can tell you, the older I get, the happier I am, and there's no way that's different for anybody.'

We drank our beer, and I forgot all about the best things in my life — or forgot to talk about them anyway — and Taryn never asked. I had been trying to think of what to say, but I guess if your life is good, and it's been good for a while, it's hard to pinpoint one thing being better than the next. I knew we were going to the party, because after twelve empty beer cans, nobody would go home.

I drove us back to the house with the mattress and the toilet out front, and as we pulled up, I saw two men sitting outside, smoking.

'That's Status and Cousin Kenny,' said Taryn.

'Do they know I'm with you?'

'Sure. Status saw your car earlier and said it was a piece of junk.'

'Tell him so is his house,' I said, turning off the ignition.

Taryn hopped out of the car, and I heard one of the smoking men call her fat as she ran by, straight into the house, leaving me standing there with the two of them. They both looked at me as I got out of the car, and didn't say anything.

I reached into my pocket, looking for a cigarette, but the pack was empty.

'Can I have one?' I asked, to either of them, as I walked up.

The one on the left had to be Status, because the other one had a mechanic's shirt on with 'Kenny' sewn into it. Status handed me a Parliament after he'd lit it off the end of his own.

'Heard you're being a good mom to Taryn,' said Cousin Kenny, and laughed a little, his head cocked to the side.

I drew in on the cigarette and looked straight at him.

'What's that supposed to mean?' I asked.

'How old are you? I bet you're older than all of us,' he said.

I took another drag and leaned over to ash in the empty bottle at Status's feet.

'Listen, you little shit,' I said. 'I'm nobody's mom, and if I was, I'd be a better one than whoever raised your sorry ass. Great fucking party, by the way.'

I threw the cigarette on the ground and turned to walk back to the car. I heard him call me a bitch, and the front door slam.

'Where are you going?' I heard Taryn call, and I heard the sound of the pine straw crunch under her feet as she ran after me toward my piece of junk car.

'Don't know,' I said, turning around. 'But I'm not staying here.'

'Okay,' she said.

'Let's go somewhere. I'll take you to a bar,' I said.

'All right. But I don't have any more money.'

'Just get in.'

Taryn rolled her window down as we pulled out of the driveway, and waved at the two men. Neither of them waved back.

'You didn't tell me the awesome things in your life,' she said, lighting a cigarette.

'And you didn't talk about your child being one of the best things in yours,' I said, and I don't even know why I said it, because until then I didn't give a damn about her kid.

Taryn didn't say anything, and she stared out the car window.

'I didn't tell you all five,' she said. 'But Lymon's not one of them. He was a mistake.'

'You're selfish,' I said.

'I couldn't think of a fifth thing. I tried, but I couldn't think of one, so that's why I didn't tell you the fifth best thing that's happened to me. And that ain't really selfish.'

'Well, I can't think of a single one,' I said, 'so four out of five doesn't seem so bad.'

'I know Lymon'll be the fifth thing, you know, but not yet. I can't say it now, if it's not true. I hope he will be. But right now I still feel like the babysitter, and most of the time I want him to go away.'

She kept staring out the window, looking into the side mirror at herself, smoking.

'It won't be like that when you're older. All of these things won't matter, and you'll be glad you have him.'

'You talk to me like a mom,' she said. 'It's annoying.'

'Have you eaten today?' I asked.

'No.'

'That's what we'll do then. I'll make you some fried chicken,' I said.

'I'd rather drink beer. I'm not hungry.'

She turned away from the mirror, from her reflection, and I knew she was looking at me. I could feel her staring as I kept my own gaze straight ahead on the road.

'Not right now, you aren't,' I said, steering the car onto the highway, 'but you will be.'

CONTRIBUTING
AUTHORS

Ericka Duffy was born and raised in Southern Ontario. Presently, she lives in Edinburgh.

Andrew Philip was born in Aberdeen in 1975 and grew up near Falkirk. He lived in Berlin for a short spell in the 1990s before studying linguistics at the University of Edinburgh. He now lives in Linlithgow and works part-time for the Scottish Parliament's official report. *The Ambulance Box*, his first book of poems, is published by Salt. He blogs at http://www.andrewphilip.net/

Jane Griffiths was born in Exeter, but brought up in Holland. She has worked as a bookbinder, lexicographer, and university lecturer in Norfolk, London, Oxford, Edinburgh, and now Bristol. Her academic publications include *John Skelton and Poetic Authority: Defining the Liberty to Speak* (Oxford University Press, 2006). She received an Eric Gregory award for her poetry in 1996. Her most recent collection, *Another Country: New & Selected Poems* (Bloodaxe, 2008), was shortlisted for the Forward Prize.

Spencer Thompson resides in Portland, Oregon with a cat named No-name. A graduate of the University of Edinburgh's creative writing program, he is currently writing a novel. He wishes to assure readers that no pancakes were harmed in this story. Spencer sailed as a merchant mariner for a decade, and carries on these age-old rowdy traditions on land. He enjoys facts, especially facts that he has made up.

Julia Boll is one of the three editors of *newleaf* magazine. She graduated from Bremen University in 2005 and is now a postgraduate student at the University of Edinburgh, where she happily recruits new authors for *newleaf*. Refusing to give in to the fact that she and her favourite literary magazine now reside in two different countries, she has taken to skyping with *nl* HQ whenever possible and can often be seen in internet cafés in the Scottish capital babbling editorial gibberish down her headset. Writing is one of her greatest passions, rivalled only by editing and, er, talking loud and fast.

Gloria Dawson was born in 1985. She won the Ledbury Poetry Prize in 2001, was a Foyle Young Poet of the Year in 2004, was shortlisted for an Eric Gregory Award in 2005 and is widely published online and in print. She has supported Jackie Kay at the Soho Theatre in London, performed in an improv jazz group in Cambridge and tottered drunkenly on the stage at the Forest Café. And read poems there, too. She is currently starting to make films and grows backwards toward toddlerhood, interested in everything, grabbing nearby objects, and Wandering Off.

Benjamin Morris is completing his PhD in Archaeology at the University of Cambridge. Previously educated at Duke University and the University of Edinburgh, his creative work appears in such places as *Seam*, *Chapman*, *Oxford Poetry*, *the Independent on Sunday*, *the Scottish Review of Books*, and the *Mays* anthologies, and has won such awards as a Pushcart nomination, a Commendation in the National Poetry Competition, the Brewer Hall Prize and the Chancellor's Medal for Poetry from Cambridge. Recently he co-edited the anthology *Stolen Stories* (Forest Publications, 2008). His preferred drink is bourbon and rocks.

Jason Morton was born a ne'er-do-well Michigander and continues this proud tradition in his adopted home of Edinburgh. He currently works as a journalist for *The Skinny* and contributes to various Forest Publications projects.

Kapka Kassabova was born in Bulgaria and educated by her scientist parents, the French College in Sofia, and two New Zealand universities. In 1990, her family emigrated to England, and later to New Zealand. During her twelve years in New Zealand, Kapka had year-long stints in France and Germany, but five years ago she moved back to Britain and now lives in Edinburgh as a happy cultural mongrel. Kapka's travel memoir of her Cold War childhood and post-communism, *Street Without a Name: childhood and other misadventures in Bulgaria*, came out in Britain, New Zealand and Bulgaria last year, and will be out in the USA this summer. It was chosen by Jan Morris as her book of the year in the *Financial Times*. Kapka's two poetry collections are *Someone else's life* (2003) and *Geography for the Lost* (2007), both with Bloodaxe. In the last years Kapka has focused heavily on travel writing. Her travel essays were twice recipients of the NZ Cathay Pacific Travel Writer of the Year award. She writes the occasional travel guide and contributes with articles and book reviews to the *Guardian*, the *Sunday Times*, *Vogue*, the *TLS*, and the *NZ Listener*.

Alan Gillis was born in Belfast and currently lives in Scotland, where he is a lecturer in English at the University of Edinburgh. His first book of poetry *Somebody, Somewhere* (Gallery Press, 2004) was shortlisted for the Irish Times Award and won The Rupert and Eithne Strong Award for Best First Collection in 2005. His second book, *Hawks and Doves* (Gallery Press, 2007), was a Poetry Book Society Recommendation and was shortlisted for the TS Eliot Prize. As a critic, he is author of *Irish Poetry of the 1930s* (Oxford University Press, 2005) and is currently co-editing *The Oxford Handbook of Modern Irish Poetry*.

Kona Macphee was born in London in 1969 and grew up in Australia, where she flirted with a range of occupations including composer, violinist, waitress and motorcycle mechanic. Eventually she took up robotics and computer science, which brought her to Cambridge as a graduate student in 1995. She now lives in the small town of Crieff, Scotland. Kona received an Eric Gregory Award for her poetry in 1998. Her first collection, *Tails*, was published by Bloodaxe in 2004, and her second collection, *Perfect Blue*, is due out in 2010.

Phil Harrison is a writer/filmmaker/designer currently straddling Edinburgh, Belfast and Cape Town. Nice work if you can get it. "The birds, like" is one of a series of short stories he is working on set in contemporary, post-Troubles Belfast, and is currently being turned into a short film. He is presently working on a feature script influenced by, among other things, Frantz Fanon's *The Wretched of the Earth*.

Nick Holdstock's work has appeared in the *Edinburgh Review*, *Stand* and *The Southern Review*. www.nickholdstock.com

Aiko Harman is a Los Angeles native, currently in Scotland pursuing an MSc in Creative Writing at the University of Edinburgh. Prior to moving across the pond, Aiko lived in Japan, teaching English to Japanese high school students. Her poetry is in *Read This* and *Fuselit*, among others. She is a recipient of the William Hunter Sharpe memorial scholarship, and winner of the 2009 Grierson Verse Prize.

Russell Jones (b.1984) grew up in Telford, England. He later studied English Literature at Lancaster University and then went on to the University of Edinburgh to practice writing poetry. Jones' work has won recognition in several poetry competitions including the Grierson Verse Prize (2007), the Bridport Prize (2007, 2008), the Eric Gregory Award (2007) and a number of national competitions. He is currently researching 'The Science Fiction Poetry of Edwin Morgan' at the University of Edinburgh.

Robert Alan Jamieson is an Edinburgh-based writer, originally from Shetland. "The Commissioners Investigate" is an extract from his fourth novel, *H-A-P-P-Y-Land*, to be published in 2010.

Jane Flett lives in Edinburgh, where she writes stories about misfits, drinks too much Scotch, runs an underground music venue, and dances really, really well. Last year she read to acclaim and whooping in Paris, Oxford, London, Cambridge and the Edinburgh International Book Festival. Find her words in *Neon*, *Johnny America*, *Ducts* and *Spindle*.

Claire Askew is the editor in chief of arts magazine *Read This*, and also runs the *Read This* poetry micropress and *One Night Stanzas*, an advice blog for poets who are just starting out. Her own work has featured in the *Edinburgh Review*, *The Glasgow Review*, *Poetry Scotland* and the Poetry Society's *Poetry News*, among others. In 2008, Claire was awarded the Grierson Verse Prize, the Sloan Prize for Writing in Lowland Scots Vernacular, the Lewis Edwards Award for Poetry and the William Hunter Sharpe Memorial Scholarship. Her first pamphlet collection is due from Red Squirrel Press in 2009. She lives in Edinburgh and works as an English lecturer at Telford College.

Ryan Van Winkle is the Reader in Residence at the Scottish Poetry Library. Recently his poems have appeared in *New Writing Scotland: 26* and *Northwords Now*. Ryan lives in Edinburgh and is a member of the Forest Arts Collective. His website is: www.ryanvanwinkle.com

Lindsay Bower currently lives in Charleston, South Carolina, after having lived in Edinburgh for the past four years. She was a past contributor to *V: New International Writing from Edinburgh* and *Stolen Stories*, and continues to write freelance for various publications. She is currently at work on a collection of short stories, and is happy to report that life in the South is as simultaneously awkward and inspiring as it was before she left.

CONTRIBUTING
MUSICIANS

Billy Liar plays acoustic guitar with a punk fury. His latest EP, *It Starts Here*, is out now and is available online or at fine petrol stations everywhere.

www.myspace.com/billyliarmusic

Vadoinmessico are Giorgio Poti (guitar and vocals), Salvador Garza (melodica, glockenspiel, keyboards and backing vocals) and Stephan B (banjo, percussion, keyboards and backing vocals). If Frankie and Annette's Beach Party also featured the arboretum scene from Sabrina, the soundtrack would be 'Cave.' Vadoinmessico creates cinematically charming songs that seem more epic than their three minutes.

www.myspace.com/vadoinmessicoband

Mat Riviere likes drones and shouting. He lives in constant fear that the bottom-of-the-range Yamaha sampler he got for his 15th birthday will one day just stop working.

www.myspace.com/matriviere

The Tuberians are an Edinburgh collective guided by the double bass of Martin Beer. They perform the compositions of Kim Tebble. Flute, saxophone, accordion and ukelele accompany stories of intergalactic travel, deserted farms and lonely love. Meet awkward chumps, distant space women and weird maidens. Their song included here, about the first Old

Tuberians' arrival on the surface, features Kim Tebble and Hailey Beavis (lead vocals), Pockets and Laura Marlow (backing vocals), Rebecca Howard and Julian Smith (clarinets), Brian Tipa (guitar & producer) and Adam Reid (drums). You can find the video on Youtube.

www.myspace.com/tuberians
www.tuberians.co.uk

Bob Hillary & the Massive Mellow is a band based around the songs of Bob Hillary, formerly lead singer and frontman for The Ruffness. The first album *Nature's Pace* is being released in 2009 with a summer tour of British festivals to follow. Live, the band play dancey grooves, resulting in a mellow upbeat positive sound that aims to get people on their feet dancin; trancey and perfect for festivals. The Massive Mellow are: Andy Farina (acoustic bass), Andy Moore (trumpet), Danny Mullins (drums, backing vox), Bob Hillary (vocals, guitars, electronics, songs, harmonica, lap steel).

www.myspace.com/bobhillary

Black Diamond Express 'are like the fastest train of the Lehigh Valley Railroad... a nine-piece band soaked in poetry, myth and bourbon.' (Mark Edmundson, *The List*). The Black Diamond Express live and perform in Edinburgh.

www.myspace.com/theblackdiamondexpress

Asazi Space Funk Explosion came together in the summer of 2003 in a dark basement in Camden. Kholeho 'Asazi' Mosala's rabble-rousing vocals and traditional South African percussion melded with Alex Marten's spacey, dubbed-out keys and skanking guitar FX. They moved to Edinburgh where they were joined by Andrew Farina on bass and Caroline Anthony on drums. A string of legendary, packed-out gigs at Edinburgh's Jazz Bar, Bongo Club, Forest Café and at the Knockengorroch Festival in Dumfriesshire have solidified their fan base.

www.asazispacefunkexplosion.com

Kevin Molloy is a writer and singer of songs, vacillating between the silly and the semi-serious. He is a very big fan of words. He hosts the monthly gig night IKTOMS in London.

www.kevinmolloy.co.uk

www.myspace.com/kevinmolloy

Sarazin Blake sings, writes, and strums songs of lost loves, bicycles, old hotels, politics and long hot drives. He has rambled coast to coast singing in basements, bars, backyards, and holding cells. He currently has seven full-length albums, two in the works, and is about to catch a train for a gig.

www.sameroomrecords.com

Skeleton Bob writes songs about Glasgow that sound like they're about America; songs about girls who did us wrong/proud; songs about The Doublet, and yes, songs about wanting to be Merle Haggard. The songs will no doubt become significantly better when Jody does, in fact, become Merle. The trio, comprising of drummer Eilidh Rodgers, bassist Richie Henderson and singer/guitarist Jody Henderson, hope to soothe your trodden heart with a filthy-sweet sound that's been likened to Uncle Tupelo, The Handsome Family, Evan Dando, and The Jesus and Mary Chain.

www.myspace.com/therealskeletonbob

Diddley Squat asks 'why are band biogs written by the band in the 3rd person?' To big oneself up, while seeming modest? Who cares! I, unnamed fraction of Diddley Squat think we're okay, great actually and proud to say it. Destroy convention, mindless pretention. We sacreligiously mix styles, bouncing around and shouting like 8 year olds on too much sugar. We love it, come see us live!

www.myspace.com/bodiddleysquat

Robin Grey makes music in a small white room with a blue door tucked away in a leafy corner of Hackney. Inspired by the timeless work of Bob Dylan and Leonard Cohen amongst many others, he colours in his songs with guitar, banjo, ukulele, mandolin, piano, percussion toys and any other instruments he can afford and fit into his little studio.

www.robingrey.com

Mammoth is a rap duo comprised of DK and Scrapdog. The two cartoonists and inter-dimensional visionaries have been writing and recording music since 1996. They've released two albums, 'The Flexible Dime' and 'Octapoc.' They rap about things that are affecting young people today — like aliens, vampires, nuclear war, and Hell.

www.johncrave.com

Groaner & Heid is the recent amalgamation of Groaner (www.myspace.com/filthygroaner) and Heid (Craig Bayne). They are far, far too enigmatic to elaborate any further.

Jonny Berliner sings songs about crustaceans, exhaustion and glucose. He has composed science songs for the *Guardian*'s Science Weekly podcast and hosts the monthly Folkadot music nights at the Green Note in Camden.

www.myspace.com/folkadot
jonnyberliner.com

Poor Edward is the moniker of Edinburgh-based singer-songwriter Sam Siggs. When playing live Poor Edward consists not only of one person (not called Edward), but a second (called J), who can make his guitar sound like a cello, a seagull, an elephant… anything you want. Poor Edward likes to play gigs and has done so with an assortment of lovely people and bands.

www.myspace.com/edwardpoor

Francois & The Atlas Mountains augment their trademark DIY set-up with striking arrangements of harp, melodica, clarinet and brass. This Glasgow-based band is almost orchestral in musical flair and subtlety.

www.kidfrancois.com

Chandra is a singer, songwriter, guitarist, choir leader, music workshop facilitator, freelance community musician, traveller and student of life.

www.myspace.com/moontravels

Jack Richold with **Faith Nicholson**: the sea-breeze stirring your hair. Haunting and heartfelt darkfolk. This song Lorca didn't write was described by Edinburgh blogger Song by Toad as 'Bloody gorgeous' and 'utterly beautiful.' Jack and Faith are now playing together as The Sea is Salt.

www.myspace.com/jackrichold

Withered Hand is the Edinburgh-based musician and artist Dan Willson. He composes most of his semi-autobiographical urban folk songs alone but prefers to perform live versions with friends. 2009 will see the release of the first Withered Hand album on SL Records, mixed and mastered by legendary American producer Kramer (Bongwater, Low, Galaxie 500) and featuring the talents of such local luminaries as Jo Foster (Fence Collective) and Meursault.

www.myspace.com/witheredhandmusic
www.slrecords.net

WHAT IS THE FOREST?

The Forest is a volunteer-run, collectively owned and operated arts charity based in the heart of Edinburgh. Self-funded by its vegetarian café, The Forest houses a gig space and art gallery, numerous workshops and the monthly Golden Hour reading and performance night. It provides an alternative space, free and open to all, to hold events, display art, make books and records, or just hang out, eat healthy food and meet like-minded individuals.

This book is one example of what The Forest funds. It also distributes grants to meritorious artistic and community projects. For more information, or to get involved, please visit The Forest in person or at our website: www.theforest.org.uk.

ALSO FROM FOREST PUBLICATIONS

November 2008
£5.99

Never, ever trust a writer.

They cluck and nod and listen and then three months later they splash your tragedy/foolishness/very embarrassing incident involving a raspberry jelly and a pair of warm curling tongs over the tawdry pages of a literary quarterly.

We feel there is no shame in this.

Quite the opposite: we believe this ugly fact deserves to be celebrated with all the pomp and hullaballoo we can possibly muster. Therefore we have compiled an anthology of the finest **Stolen Stories** — a collection of sixteen tales from both established and emerging thieves, all of whom have been forced to confess the source of their thefts.

We feel that it is time to be honest: *This* is where our ideas come from.

August 2007
£7.00

The Golden Hour is poetry and prose, it's acoustic and it's electric, it's physical and mental. **The Golden Hour Book** (and CD) is an effort to distil the goodness of our live performance — the words, the music, the bottles of beer and wine — into a volume of pure, unrefined Gold featuring the artists who performed over the first year of The Golden Hour. It is Golden.

This first volume of collected stories, poetry and songs from The Golden Hour captures new and fresh international voices.

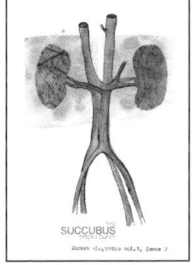

The **Forest Chapbook Series** offers bite-sized monthly instalments of prose and poetry in artistic quality packaging for only £2 each.

Each issue in the series will feature a different voice telling a new story, with launches happening at the monthly Golden Hour night at the Forest Café.

CD TRACKLIST

1. Billy Liar, 'It Starts Here'
2. Vadoinmessico, 'Cave'
3. Mat Riviere, 'FYH'
4. The Tuberians, 'Tuberians Have Landed'
5. Bob Hilary & The Massive Mellow, 'Hear Mi'
6. The Black Diamond Express, 'Jack'
7. Asazi Space Funk Explosion, 'Syababona'
8. Kevin Molloy, 'Goddess Of The Rain'
9. Sarazin Blake, 'India Or Spain'
10. Skeleton Bob, 'Love Song'
11. Diddley Squat, 'Camel Song'
12. Robin Grey, 'Women'
13. Mammoth, 'Sunshine'
14. Groaner & Heid, 'Massive Genius'
15. Jonny Berliner, 'Kneeling Down'
16. Poor Edward, 'Children Of Little Or No Importance'
17. Francois & The Atlas Mountains, 'I'm So Glad I Met You'
18. Chandra, 'Malaika'
19. Jack Richold with Faith Nicholson, 'Lady Of The Calico'
20. Withered Hand, 'Takeaway Food'